COMPARATIVE POLITICS

Political Institutions

COMPARATIVE POLITICS

Comparative Politics is a series for students and teachers of political science that deals with contemporary issues in comparative government and politics. As Comparative European Politics it has produced a series of high-quality books since its foundation in 1990, but now takes on a new form and a new title for the millennium—Comparative Politics. As the process of globalization proceeds, and as Europe becomes ever more enmeshed in world trends and events, so it is necessary to broaden the scope of the series.

The General Editors are Max Kaase, Vice President and Dean of Humanities and Social Sciences, International University, Bremen, and Kenneth Newton, Professor of Comparative Politics, University of Southampton. The series is published in association with the European Consortium for Political Research.

RECENT TITLES IN THE SERIES

Mixed-Member Electoral Systems: The Best of Both Worlds
Edited by Matthew Shugart and Martin P. Wattenberg

Parties without Partisans: Political Change in Advanced Industrial Democracies
Edited by Russell J. Dalton and Martin P. Wattenberg

Coalition Governments in Western Europe
Edited by Wolfgang C. Müller and Kaare Strøm

Divided Government in Comparative Perspective
Edited by Robert Elgie

Political Parties: Old Concepts and New Challenges
Edited by Richard Gunther, José Ramón Montero, and Juan J. Linz

Parliamentary Representatives in Europe 1848–2000: Legislative Recuitment and Careers in Eleven European Countries
Edited by Heinrich Best and Maurizio Cutta

Political Parties in the New Europe: Political and Analytical Challenges
Edited by Kurt Richard Luther and Ferdinand Müller-Rommel

Political Institutions

Democracy and Social Choice

JOSEP M. COLOMER

OXFORD
UNIVERSITY PRESS

This book has been printed digitally and produced in a standard specification in order to ensure its continuing availability

OXFORD
UNIVERSITY PRESS

Great Clarendon Street, Oxford OX2 6DP

Oxford University Press is a department of the University of Oxford.
It furthers the University's objective of excellence in research, scholarship,
and education by publishing worldwide in

Oxford New York

Auckland Cape Town Dar es Salaam Hong Kong Karachi
Kuala Lumpur Madrid Melbourne Mexico City Nairobi
New Delhi Shanghai Taipei Toronto
With offices in
Argentina Austria Brazil Chile Czech Republic France Greece
Guatemala Hungary Italy Japan South Korea Poland Portugal
Singapore Switzerland Thailand Turkey Ukraine Vietnam

Oxford is a registered trade mark of Oxford University Press
in the UK and in certain other countries

Published in the United States
by Oxford University Press Inc., New York

Oxford is a registered trade mark of Oxford University Press
in the UK and in certain other countries

Published in the United States
by Oxford University Press Inc., New York

© Josep Colomer 2001

The moral rights of the author have been asserted

Database right Oxford University Press (maker)

Reprinted 2006

All rights reserved. No part of this publication may be reproduced,
stored in a retrieval system, or transmitted, in any form or by any means,
without the prior permission in writing of Oxford University Press,
or as expressly permitted by law, or under terms agreed with the appropriate
reprographics rights organization. Enquiries concerning reproduction
outside the scope of the above should be sent to the Rights Department,
Oxford University Press, at the address above

You must not circulate this book in any other binding or cover
And you must impose this same condition on any acquirer

ISBN 0-19-924184-8

Preface

The more complex the political institutions, the more stable and socially efficient the outcomes will be. This book develops an extensive analysis of this relationship. The discussion is theoretical, historical, and comparative. Concepts, questions, and insights are based on social choice theory, while an empirical focus is cast on about forty countries and a few international organizations from late medieval times to the present.

Political institutions are conceived here as the formal rules of the game, especially with respect to the following issues: who can vote, how votes are counted, and what is voted for. Complexity signifies that multiple winners exist, as in plural electorates created by broad voting rights, in multiparty systems based upon proportional representation, and in frameworks of division of powers between the executive and the legislative or between the central government and noncentral units. The efficiency of outcomes is evaluated for their social utility, which is to say, the aggregation of individuals' utility which is obtained with the satisfaction of their preferences.

This is a book that emphasizes the advantages of median voter's cabinets and presidents, divided government, and federalism. It differs from certain arguments developed in other pluralistic traditions in giving the emphasis to the role of institutional rules and decision procedures in the production of different degrees of citizens' political satisfaction, rather than to the predispositions created by social, economic, or cultural structures. Political pluralism is not either praised here for the sake of itself or only as a means for limiting power, as in certain constructions aimed at preserving individual freedom above all. Pluralistic democratic institutions are judged to be better than alternative formulas for their higher capacity of producing socially satisfactory results.

J.M.C.

Acknowledgements

This book was mostly written during my stays at New York University, Georgetown University, and the Institute of Political Studies of Paris during the years 1995–9. I am particularly grateful to my sponsors in the three institutions, Steven Brams, Eusebio Mujal-León, and Jean Léca, respectively. Partial drafts were presented to the graduate students in the mentioned institutions, as well as at the Graduate Conference of Swiss Universities held in Cully, Switzerland, the Latin American Faculty of Social Sciences (FLACSO), and the Center of Research for Development (CIDAC), in Mexico, the University Sanmartín in Buenos Aires and the University Siglo 21 in Córdoba (Argentina), the University of Costa Rica, the University Rafael Landívar in Guatemala, and the University of Panamá.

Among those who provided unavailable data, created occasions of exchanges or made useful comments, I should mention Antonio Agosta, Manuel Alcántara, Alberto Alesina, Gerard Alexander, Klaus Armingeon, John Bailey, Michel Balinski, Samuel Barnes, Michelle Beyeler, Carles Boix, Ana-Sofía Cardenal, Marcelo Cavarozzi, Grace-Ivana Deheza, Alberto Díaz-Cayeros, Patrick Dunleavy, Lars Feld, Peter Fishburn, Bernard Grofman, José-Luis de Haro, Erick Hess, Evelyn Huber, Robert Lieber, Arend Lijphart, Juan Linz, Iain McLean, Beatriz Magaloni, Helen Margetts, Nicholas Miller, Gianfranco Pasquino, Stanley Payne, Rubén-Darío Rodríguez-Patiño, Donald Saari, Ignacio Sánchez-Cuenca, Giulia de Sanctis, Manfred Schmidt, Matthew Shugart, Ligia Tavera, Arturo Valenzuela, and Stephen Wayne. Thanks to Georgetown University, I could rely upon two research assistants, Francesca Vassallo and Eric Langenbacher, and the editing services of Sarah Campbell.

I also enjoyed working with the series co-editor, Ken Newton, and Oxford University Press editor Dominic Byatt. Financial help was provided by the Boards of Scientific and Technological Research of the Government of Spain (CICYT, PR95-249) and of the Government of Catalonia (CIRIT, 1995BEAI400127).

Contents

List of Figures

List of Tables

1

Politics and Social Choice

> What is the best regime and the best way of life for most citizens and most human beings?
> The political community that is based on those in the middle is best. The best legislators come from the middle citizens. . . .
> The better mixed the polity is, the more lasting it is.
>
> Aristotle, *The Politics* (*c.* 325–324 BC)

The stake of politics is the provision of public goods by leaders. By definition, public goods cannot be provided by private actors unless they are submitted to the appropriate institutional constraints, which implies the embodiment of some political structure. Political leaders may also provide private goods, but this does not distinguish them from other social actors.

Politics always involves exchanges between leaders and citizens to their mutual benefit. The essential exchange is between leaders providing public goods and citizens giving leaders their support or their votes. While public goods can satisfy some citizen groups' common interests, citizens' support to leaders is transformed into opportunities for staying in power, obtaining private goods, acquiring fame, or developing a professional political career.

Some rivalry or competition between different institutional providers of public goods may exist in situations of civil war or in transitory situations of regime change. But public goods are market failures and can be provided effectively only by a monopoly, thus requiring a clear delimitation of every provider's domain. The role of the institutions is to establish the domains of public activity and the rules to select leaders. (For a formal discussion, see Colomer 1995*b*.)

This basic scheme can be valid for all types of political regimes, whether democratic or not. Some authoritarian regimes may find social support on the basis of delivering certain public goods, whether they be social peace and order, national pride and foreign expansion, or some positive economic performance. However, the smaller the number of people participating in the appointment of leaders and in the decision making, the higher the likelihood that only private good interests or small groups' public interests will be satisfied with policy decisions. Nondemocratic or self-appointed rulers will tend to satisfy the common interests of themselves and their supporters, while resisting the demands of other groups by restrictive mechanisms or repressive means. Conversely, the greater the number of individuals participating in electing leaders and decision making, the greater the opportunities for large groups to develop their demands and be satisfied by policy outcomes.

Ideally, democracy could be defined as the rule of the many in their common interests. Yet public goods can be the subject of democratic competition because all of them involve some redistributive dimension. Certain public goods can be considered to be universal, satisfying very large common interests because they can benefit all citizens in ways they can hardly anticipate. This category may include goods such as defense, security, justice, a constitutional provision for balanced budgets, or environmental protection. Universal public goods may be provided through consensual policies, even in relatively restrictive regimes. Yet even these goods can be provided by policies producing different amounts of citizens' satisfaction and social utility. This is the case, for example, with defense based on either the draft or a professional army. A budget surplus can produce some universal benefits, including low inflation, but it benefits citizens differently depending on whether it is spent in defense, social security, or in any other field. Taxpayers' money can be used to fund either a state-controlled school system or religious schools, although both can satisfy a universal right to go to school. Public works involve choices on location, externalities, and so forth.

Different institutional formulas perform with different degrees of social efficiency in the provision of public goods. In other words, social choices corresponding to different institutional procedures of decision making satisfy different groups of citizens' demands and produce different levels of social utility. Specifically, democratic regimes organized in simple institutional frameworks foster the concentration of power and alternation of successive absolute winners and absolute losers. They favor political satisfaction of relatively small groups, as well as policy instability. In contrast, pluralistic institutions produce multiple winners, inducing multiparty cooperation and agreements. They favor stable, moderate, and consensual policies that can satisfy large groups' interests on a great number of issues.

1.1. THE THEORY OF SOCIAL CHOICE

Social choice theory has developed a research program that touches the core of the study of politics. The founding theorems demolished a naive confidence in the capability of political institutions to guarantee efficient outcomes satisfying citizens' preferences. No decision rule can guarantee outcomes fulfilling some apparently simple requirements of fairness, but all of them are vulnerable to manipulation by voters and leaders and may produce socially inefficient results, according to the 'impossibility theorems' established by Kenneth Arrow (1951, 1963), Duncan Black (1948*a*, *b*, 1958), Allan Gibbard (1973), and Mark Satterwhaite (1975), among others.

Three basic routes from this starting point can be distinguished. First, some of the normative conditions initially established to declare a social choice acceptable have been discussed and relaxed. The corresponding proposals focus on the following conditions: (i) monotonicity, or the requirement of a consistent relation between citizens' preferences and the social choice; (ii) independence of the social choice from individual preferences regarding irrelevant alternatives that cannot win the voting contest; and (iii) a new interpretation of the condition initially called 'no-dictatorship' in order to make the existence of a (nonautomatically) decisive actor acceptable (e.g., Sen 1970; Barberà 1977; Dowding 1997, respectively, for the three conditions mentioned). These contributions usually help the student to mistrust his or her own ethical intuition and to follow reasonable discussions of normative criteria. Yet they also show that any choice of conditions of fairness requires renouncing some possible criterion of value, or at least accepting a trade-off between several of them, which finally depends on subjective judgement.

Second, certain conditions regarding citizens' preferences have been identified in order to guarantee efficient and stable social choices with certain voting procedures. This line of research relaxes the founding theorems' assumption that no restrictions should be imposed on individuals' preferences (or 'universal domain'). The alternative conditions, such as 'single-peakedness' of individual preference curves (Black 1958), 'values restriction' (Sen 1966), and 'extremes restriction' (Sen and Pattanaik 1969), suggest the advantages of relatively homogeneous societies in producing stable and consistent collective decisions. Yet, as will be discussed in the following pages, the restriction of relevant preferences may result from the decision process itself, ultimately depending on the institutional rules of the game.

The third line of research promoted by social choice theory—and the one most closely connected to this book—attempts to evaluate the relative performance of different institutional rules in satisfying citizens' preferences and producing socially efficient outcomes. The 'impossibility' theorems tell us that it is impossible to guarantee stable and efficient social choices with any rule. But the point is not only that it is 'possible' to obtain stable and socially efficient choices with some rules, but also that certain rules produce inefficient choices more frequently than others. In a world of uncertainty, the likelihood of social efficiency may be a useful guide to institutional evaluation and design.

The Study of Political Institutions

The basic perspective adopted in this book is that political institutions shape actors' strategies, and that the latter produce collective outcomes. Institutions provide information, opportunities, incentives, and constraints for both citizens and leaders choosing certain strategies, and it is only through the intermediation of actors' strategic decisions that collective outcomes can be explained.

Debts must be acknowledged, in particular, to certain conceptual contributions dealing with the choice of institutions, the incentives they supply for different strategies, their effects on the outcomes, and the advantages of pluralistic institutions, respectively.

First, Douglass North's theory of 'equilibrium institutions' remarks that the choice and the survival of institutions depend on their performance in providing public goods and reducing transaction costs, as well as on the path by which they are chosen, including the role of small events and luck in gaining adherence. Once institutions exist, they set parameters for further action. But they can also reinforce themselves and make their replacement difficult through the effects of the incentives embodied in their structure. Even certain institutions producing inefficient outcomes can survive as a consequence of actors' learning by use, their adaption to institutional regularities, and the costs of their replacement (North and Thomas 1973; North 1990*a*, *b*).

The varied panorama of democratic institutional formulas that will parade before the eyes of the reader of this book may be, perhaps, the most persuasive empirical evidence of the variety of equilibrium institutions. Yet, risk-adverse rulers submitted to the challenge of alternative potential winners may choose to change the rules of the game in order to minimize their losses. Also, permanent losers under the existing institutions may try to replace them with other devices favoring wider distribution of power. On this basis, some historical patterns in favor of choosing pluralistic institutions will be identified.

Second, William Riker's seminal exploration of 'heresthetics' has led political students to resuming the classical and too-long forgotten concern with the art of making decisions under given institutional rules. According to this approach, political strategy may consist of such activities as setting the agenda with a particular selection of issues, giving prominence to certain evaluative dimensions of the available alternatives in the public debate, or voting insincerely in order to obtain a more satisfactory collective result (Riker 1983, 1986, 1993, 1996*b*). The corresponding question explored in this book is how different institutional formulas may favor different strategies and how permissive each of them may be for manipulative actions.

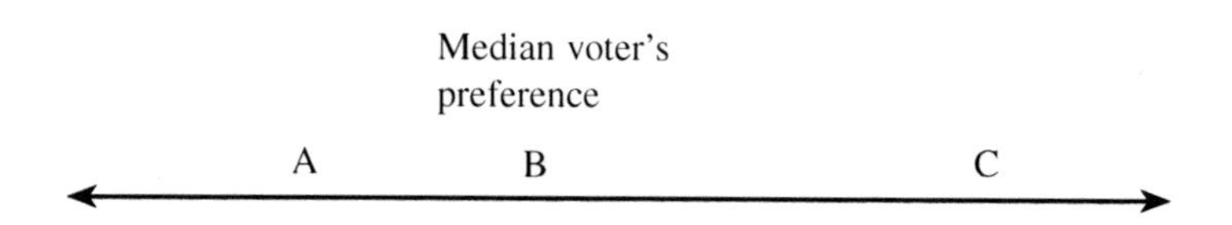

FIG. 1.1. The single-dimensional electorate (N = three voters: A, B, C)

federalism. If significant groups of voters have a different intensity of preferences on various issues and they can vote on them separately, they can find considerable satisfaction in institutional schemes producing different winners on different issues. Under this assumption, social utility can be maximized if different issue domains are allocated to different institutions according to the distribution of intensity of preferences among voters. Also, interinstitutional cooperation can lead to compromise, intermediate decisions supported by broad, consensual majorities producing wide political satisfaction.

A Model of Social Choice

A simple geometrical analysis can illustrate the effects of different institutional frameworks on the stability and collective utility of the social choice. Let us start with the most simple case of an electorate composed of three voters with differentiated preferences (or three voters' groups with the same preferences and a similar number of members).

Initially, we make the simple assumption that voters' preferences can be located on a single issue-dimension, such as A, B, and C on the horizontal axis in Fig. 1.1. Let us assume, for instance, that the distance between voter A and voter B is half the distance between voter B and voter C, as suggested in the figure. If B, which is the median voters' preference wins, the total distance from the voters' preferences to the winner or voters' disutility can be measured as the distance from A to B, say it is 1 unit, plus the distance from B to B, which is zero, plus the distance from C to B, 2 units, so the sum of distances from voters' preferences to the winner, or total disutility, equals 3 units:

$$- U(B) = (|A - B| + |B - B| + |B - C|) = (1 + 0 + 2) = 3.$$

In contrast, if the winner were A, the sum of distances from the voters' preferences to the winner or total disutility would be 4 units; if the winner were C, the total disutility would be 5 units, as the reader can easily check. This shows that the median voter's alternative (B in the example) minimizes the sum of distances and maximizes social utility.

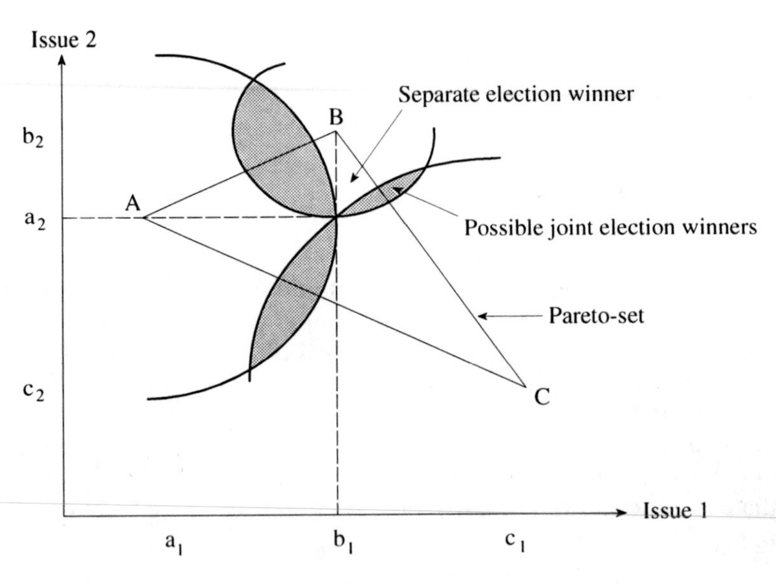

FIG. 1.2. Joint and separate elections

Note: Bold lines circumscribe the 'win-set' in a joint election on two issues (N = three voters: A, B, C)

Let us turn now to the two-dimensional case. Three voters, A, B, and C, hold different preferences on issue 1 (a_1, b_1, and c_1) and on issue 2 (a_2, b_2, and c_2), as presented in Fig. 1.2. First, we discuss the effects of separate and joint elections. Let us assume that there are two separate elections for different offices dealing with different issues or sets of issues, such as those corresponding to the two dimensions in Fig. 1.2. They can correspond, for example, to separate elections for a president focusing, say, on foreign and defense policy issues and for the Assembly focusing on economic and social policy issues, or to separate elections for two chambers in Parliament, or to other analogous institutional arrangements. Let us assume that, on each separate election, the intermediate alternative close to the median voter is advantaged and wins. In Fig. 1.2, b_1 wins in the election on issue 1 and a_2 wins in the election on issue 2. The social choice is represented by the intersection point of the winning positions on each issue, $b_1 - a_2$.

As can be seen, the social choice of separate elections on different issues under the above assumptions is a somewhat centrist point located inside the minimal set containing all voters' preferences, or the Pareto-set (the triangle A B C in the figure). This point is relatively close to the social optimum, which is the point minimizing the sum of distances from citizens' preferences and thus maximizing social utility. Precisely, in a two-dimensional space such as that in Fig. 1.2, the social optimum point is located at the intersection of the straight lines from each voter's preference to the median of the opposite side in the triangle.

Now, let us assume, alternatively, that the social choice on all the issues is made in a single election, as would correspond to a simple institutional framework, such as a unitary, unicameral parliamentary regime. The institutional setting forces the voters to choose, not between alternatives on separate issues, but between 'packages' of alternatives on all the issues at the same time.

The set of possible winners, or 'win-set', in such a joint election is unpredictable and depends on the status quo. Let us adopt the hypothesis that the status quo is the social choice previously produced by two separate elections, the point $b_1 - a_2$ in Fig. 1.2. The set of possible winners in a single, two-dimensional election from this point is represented by the multipetal shaded area in the figure. This is formed by circular indifference curves around the voters' preferences and crossing the status quo. It is assumed that every voter prefers the alternatives that are closer to the voter's preference and in particular prefers those inside the indifference curve to those outside. Accordingly, the set of possible majority winners in a joint election is formed by all the points at which a majority of voters (any majority of two voters out of three in the example shown in Fig. 1.2) is more satisfied than they would be in the status quo—that is, the win-set is formed by the intersections of pairs of indifference curves.

As can be seen, the set of possible winners in a joint election is relatively large, which makes the prediction of results difficult. The set includes many points located at a relatively long distance from the social optimum point. A number of possible winners are located outside the Pareto-set and even beyond the rank of voters' preferences (for example, the set includes some points located beyond the extreme preference, b_2, on issue 2). The possibility that many different alternatives can win may generate instability in the outcome of a series of successive elections, since any winning point can be further beaten by some other point in the corresponding win-set.

This analysis allows us to state that a joint election on a multidimensional set of issues, as a model for the typical single election in simple regimes, can be more uncertain, produce lower social utility, and be more unstable over time than separate elections on different issues, such as elections for different offices in regimes with division of powers.

The comparative judgement of separate and joint elections might be somewhat different if we replaced the assumption that the median voter's position wins in each separate election with the assumption that extreme alternatives can win (perhaps as a consequence of multiparty competition

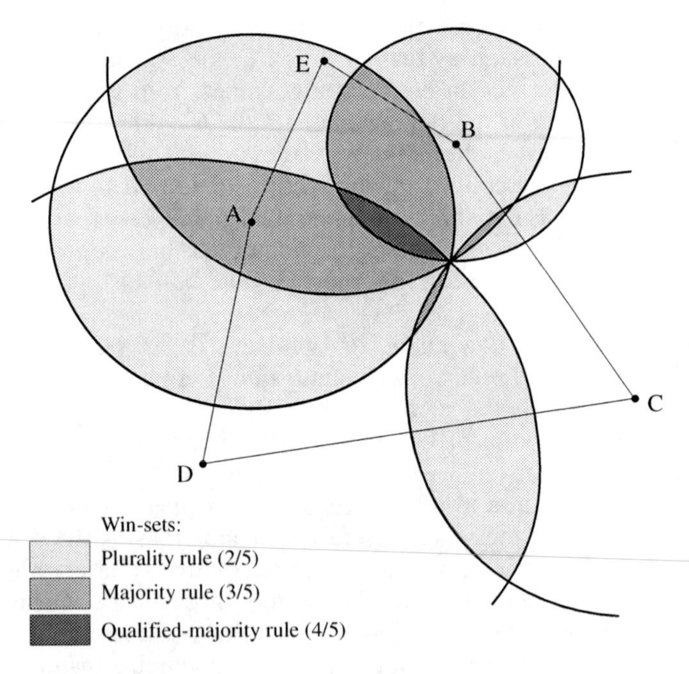

FIG. 1.3. Complex electorate with different voting rules (N = five voters: A, B, C, D, E)

with plurality rule). Still, the social choice of separate elections would always be within the rank of voters' preferences and likely inside the Pareto-set. The social choice of separate elections could be less socially efficient than some possible winners in a joint election only if extreme positions corresponding to opposite groups of extreme voters won on the different issues. But, even in this case, the set of possible winners in a joint election would include other points outside the Pareto-set and possibly some beyond the ranks of voters' preferences.

Now, we introduce two new variables in the model. First, let us assume a more complex electorate, composed of five voters with more dispersed preferences than the three previous voters. In other words, the electorate of three voters, A, B, and C, is enlarged with two new voters, D and E, whose preferences are located beyond the rank of the incumbent voters' preferences, as shown in Fig. 1.3. The addition of D and E may correspond to the enforcement of voter rights for new groups, as in a typical process of gradual democratization.

The set of possible winners in a joint election depends on the voting rule. We compare the effects of three rules with different inclusive thresholds: plurality, majority, and qualified-majority. The largest plurality is operationalized as 2/5 (or 40 per cent, not very different from the proportion of votes obtained by the typical winner in certain parliamentary elections by plurality rule in the real world).

The set of possible winners in a joint election with plurality rule for five voters is much larger than the set of winners previously identified for the electorate of three voters, as can be seen in Fig. 1.3. It includes many points located at very long distances from the social optimum point, outside the Pareto-set, and beyond the ranks of voters' preferences. This can produce high unpredictability and instability of the social choice, as well as low social utility.

The set of possible winners with majority rule (or 3/5) is shown in Fig. 1.3. As can be seen, it is smaller than the set of possible winners with plurality rule. This means that the more inclusive the decision rule, the more stable and socially efficient the social choice can be expected to be.

Comparing this result with the set of possible majority winners in the previous electorate of three voters in Fig. 1.2, the electorate of five voters can be considered to be able to produce relatively efficient results. This is not only related to the fact that a higher proportion of voters in a community can increase the sum total of individual utilities. In addition, the new set of majority winners with five voters is located mostly inside the Pareto-set, relatively closer to the social optimum point. This allows us to state that the effects of instability and possible low social utility that come with a complex electorate with highly dispersed voters' preferences may be compensated with the opposite effects produced by inclusive decision rules.

This finding is confirmed with the analysis of a qualified-majority rule, 4/5 in Fig. 1.3. The corresponding set of possible winners is the very small area in black, which is completely inside the Pareto-set and at a rather centrist location. It can certainly produce more stable social choices and higher social utility than the less inclusive rules previously analyzed.

Three institutional variables producing different degrees of stability and different amounts of utility of the social choice have been identified. In the order in which they will be analyzed in the following chapters, they are:

(i) the different degrees of dispersion of voters' preferences, corresponding to simple and complex electorates;
(ii) the inclusiveness of voting rules and decision procedures; and
(iii) the different number of issue dimensions in single and separate elections, corresponding to schemes of unity and division of powers.

This book argues that pluralistic democratic regimes based upon complex electorates, inclusive voting rules, and division of powers are likely to produce socially efficient results.

1.2. THE PLAN OF THE BOOK

The findings of the model just presented guide the research program developed in the following pages. The second chapter deals with the historical construction of simple and complex electorates through the development of different strategies in the allocation of voting rights to different groups. Arguments of both suffragists and restrictionists are revised from the perspective of the expected dispersion of voters' preferences that they were ready to promote or to accept. Three basic patterns developed in different sets of countries are distinguished for the social inclusiveness and the political stability that they were able to produce. The basic assumption is that the higher the proportion of citizens with rights to participate in a stably institutionalized political process, the higher the social utility that can be obtained

The third chapter contrasts single-winner voting rules based upon requirements of either unanimity, majority, or plurality, with multiwinner rules based upon proportional representation and multiparty coalitions. The various voting and decision rules are evaluated and compared for their inclusiveness, the relation between the outcomes that they tend to favor and the citizens' preferences, and the corresponding social utility. The different rules are submitted to a broad empirical test regarding the production of socially efficient winners corresponding to the median voter's preference.

The fourth chapter analyzes and compares different schemes of unity and division of powers which promote collective decisions on different amounts of issues at the same time. Parliamentarism, semi-presidentialism, and presidentialism, as well as unitary states and federalism, are compared by applying the categories of unified and divided government to all of them. Different formulas supply different incentives for multiparty and interinstitutional cooperation, in this way creating different opportunities for citizens' preferences to be revealed and satisfied. The emergence of multiple winners in schemes of division of powers is considered to be able to produce broadly diffused social utility.

The fifth chapter concludes with a comparison between the institutional formulas that can be considered to be the most socially efficient ones in the light of the previous analyses, including proportional representation, horizontal division of powers, and federalism, and the institutional alternatives that are mainly chosen in strategic processes of democratization and institutional reform. Self-interested but not all-powerful actors in processes of institutional change tend to choose pluralistic institutions that are considered relatively efficient in the theoretical perspective developed in this book.

The main points of the analysis, including the production of socially efficient electoral results and the frequency of divided government, are tested with data on votes, Assemblies, Cabinets, and Presidents corresponding to the outcomes of 506 national elections and 1,765 regional elections in forty democratic countries in Western and Central Europe, North and South America, and Asia, during the period 1945–2000. The countries are selected for having more than one million inhabitants, high levels of political freedom and at least two consecutive democratic elections by 2000, and available data. The countries selected include more than 90 per cent of the world population living in democracy at the end of the 20th century. The comparative analysis is complemented with a large number of brief case studies of institutional performance and change, including a few excursions several centuries ago (using sources in eight languages). The long-term historical review presented in the final chapter is supported with data on 123 major institutional changes in 85 countries during a 127-year period.

2

Who Can Vote

> The laws which establish the rights of suffrage are fundamental to democratic government.
>
> Montesquieu, *De l'Esprit des Lois* (1748)

A political community can be defined as a set of individuals who recognize some basic common interest among themselves and make enforceable collective decisions. Simple communities with concentrated preferences can make decisions relatively easily. When the bulk of the population is sufficiently homogeneous in socioeconomic and cultural terms, as usually happens in small communities, an electorate based upon broad voting rights can identify an acceptable alternative and produce a relatively stable and satisfactory social choice even without sophisticated institutional mechanisms. As will be examined below, small communities with homogeneous interests may adopt virtual universal suffrage and make decisions by unanimity or other highly inclusive voting rules.

In contrast, complex electorates formed by the enfranchisement of differentiated groups in relatively heterogeneous societies can make the achievement of enforceable collective decisions difficult and result in low degrees of stability and utility of social choice. This is usually the case in modern societies in the process of building large, initially heterogeneous nation-states, and undergoing democratization. The more dispersed the preferences of voters' groups on the issues submitted to voting, the more complex the electorate and the more difficult it is to reach agreements.

In modern historical developments, the consequences of giving voting rights to different groups in complex societies have varied enormously. The enfranchisement of certain groups has not produced much political innovation because most of their members have developed similar preferences to those already existing within the incumbent electorate and eventually replicate its voting patterns. This absence of innovation can result from some economic or personal dependence of the newly enfranchised voters upon the incumbents' preferences, or from restrictive political institutions.

Certain new voters' groups, in contrast, have been able to create new political parties, to develop eventually successful strategies to innovate the political agenda, to form a new political majority, or to challenge the ure in which the identification of a common choice was not a very cult achievement. The units in question were small territories, either ages, communes, municipalities, provinces, counties, towns, boroughs, onies, or other communities of minor size. Their collective processes decision making dealt with a few local, relatively simple issues. This s so even when they elected local representatives to larger-scale bodies, h as the medieval parliaments, due to the absence of large-scale ational') parties.

Homogeneous preferences developed among the population, reflecting her social simplicity, especially in rural environments, or the predominance of a middle class of farmers, artisans, or traders in more complex ttings. The homogeneity of the community or the strong appeal of some ocially central position allowed these communities to make enforceable ollective decisions with relative ease, producing stable, widely satisfacory social choices.

Certain institutional features of simple political communities making consensual decisions were very similar to those that can be found nowadays in meetings of condominium owners—which is another case of small, simple communities with clearly identifiable common interests. They include the following:

- Voting rights were given to the heads of households, independently on the number of family members, in the assumption that all of them had homogeneous preferences; usually only men voted, but the rules were rather vague or informal, often allowing young people or certain women to participate.
- Decision rules were highly inclusive; unanimity or quasi-unanimity rules were used in town meetings and people's assemblies that worked by acclamation.
- Several randomizing mechanisms, including turns and lots, were used for rotation of officers in charge of implementing the assembly's decisions, which was considered a burden rather than a privilege.

The election of representatives induced more innovation in favor of rules permitting a varied representation of different social categories or preference groups. Modern formulas of proportional representation were unknown at the time, but, in communities relatively more complex than the typical rural villages, interesting instances, such as multimember districts and the frequent call of elections, were conceived with the aim of preventing the exclusive rule of some particular group.

Small, somewhat homogeneous units dealing with local issues could maintain open, large participation in collective decision making by resisting pressures from large-scale Emperors, Popes, monarchs, and colonial

entire political system. This tendency toward inn
more differentiated voters' preferences and from pe
tutions.

The allocation of voting rights tends to be guic
pressures 'from below' (previously excluded groups
lations 'from above' (incumbent leaders). In moder
merchants, artisans, workers, servants, women, memb
ties, young people, and immigrants have been enfra
countries at various historical moments, usually
rearrangements in the electoral rules, the party system
tional elements.

In certain cases, universal suffrage has been introdu
without modifying previously existing institutional rule
ing high political instability. In other cases, different m
voters have been enfranchised at successive stages i
process. This strategy can prevent the sudden emergence
native majority and induce each new small group to enter i
existing party. Finally, in some cases, universal suffrage h
panied by institutional innovations, such as proportional
and division of powers, thus producing multiple electoral v
sort of new institutional framework, the social choice is
post-electoral stages in which pluralistic, inclusive agree
attained.

This chapter is divided into two sections. The first sectio
certain amount of evidence of small, homogeneous com
medieval and early modern times which were able to make
enforceable social choices by voting with relatively broad vo
The second section approaches the problems of social choice
electorates. Different historical arguments in favor of or a
enlargement of the existing electorates are revised and discusse
perspective sketched here. Different strategies in the allocation
rights are identified and associated with different enfranchiseme
electoral rules, and party systems in a dozen countries during the
20th centuries.

2.1. SIMPLE ELECTORATES

In medieval and early modern times there were not only numerous
enclaves and a few extensive imperial and monarchical structures, b
array of local units where many collective decisions were made b
vote of a large electorate. Typically, these were rather simple commun
with relatively harmonious interests, shared values, and a homogene

powers. Yet, when the traditional local communities experienced growing internal complexity and more differentiated groups emerged, their own traditional criteria in favor of broad suffrage rights and unanimous agreements became a source of conflict and instability. External trade, wider communications, and the increasing prominence of larger-scale public goods leading to the formation of modern nation-states induced major institutional rearrangements. These included the redefinition of the qualifications for voting, even including the disenfranchisement of certain voting groups, as well as more explicit regulations of elections. (For a related historical perspective, see Manin 1995.)

Cases: Communes, Parliaments, and Colonies

According to legend, the German tribal groups of the early Middle Ages held primary assemblies of warriors in which they approved resolutions offered by the king by clashing spears against shield or disapproved them by silence. The survey presented in the following pages focuses on simple electorates of three modern types of political units. First, we will approach decision making procedures in independent small communes, including the Swiss rural villages and cantons that have existed since the late Middle Ages and certain famous medieval Italian towns. The medieval commune in Central Europe was initially a private association of households organized to provide some basic public goods. They assumed the administration of justice, military defense, maintenance of a food supply, and other basic services. To the extent that the counts and the bishops were unable to perform these tasks effectively, the communes gradually replaced their authority. Eventually, they, in fact, ignored the sovereignty of the German Emperor or the Roman Pope.

Second, elections in local units within certain large kingdoms will be reviewed. They include town assemblies, provincial estates, and the Estates-General in pre-revolutionary Bourbon France, as well as counties and boroughs in parliamentary elections in Hanoverian England. Initially, the members of medieval assemblies summoned by the kings were not elected by popular constituencies, but selected from among those who were thought to be representatives of the mood and interests of diverse social categories in large territories. However, popularly elected representatives of communes or other local units also sent delegates to medieval parliaments. Modern parliamentary elections were established largely upon this precedent.

Third, some notorious colonial institutions will be discussed. They include the British dominions in North America before the formation of the United States, as well as certain Spanish colonies in North and South America in the process of attaining independence. Although based on different models, in both cases the enforcement of relatively restrictive regulations of elections in the metropolis permitted more permissive practices in the colonies located at the other side of the Atlantic. Participatory elections were in fact crucial events in triggering independence. Only when small independent units formed larger nation-states, were certain initially vague criteria of enfranchisement replaced with more specific requirements.

Evidence of the cases of simple electorates here discussed has emerged or has been recently re-elaborated among historians. But, apparently, different country cases have not been put together, or at least they have not been compared, from the perspective adopted here.

The Swiss Communes and Cantons

During the Middle Ages, German communes were recognized as the maximum legal and political authority over their rural population. They made decisions at people's assemblies with a fixed membership of the masters of households who were at least 14 or 16 years old. Married women and children were allowed passive membership and attended the meetings, but usually they did not vote, under the presumption that every house and family held homogeneous interests. Based on the commonality of private goods, the commune's membership was determined in the same way attendance to owners' meetings in modern urban condominiums is decided: only residents in the commune, and not aliens or temporary tenants without a stake in the common property, were admitted.

The assembly was called to the sound of bells, typically on Sunday morning, and gathered in a circle in a green meadow. It opened with a silent prayer. Anyone could present a proposal to the assembly. Voting was by show of hands and decisions were made by majority. The homogeneity and transparency of the community created strong incentives for attending the meetings and also for transforming a majority into unanimity. After voting, an oath of membership and obedience to the commune was taken. Other rules could be applied for other purposes: proportional partition of resources and burdens held in common, or rotation of access to public goods. Lots were used to appoint officers in charge of implementing the assembly's decisions. Cooperative action expanded among neighboring communes. Yet the homogeneity of every unit remained very high, including language, religion, and other cultural traits. Communes in which conflict became too persistent were partitioned in order to preserve the homogeneity of each decision unit.

From 1291, the little forest cantons of Uri, Schwyz, and Unterwalden began to break away from the Counts of Habsburg in Austria. Eventually, they formed a league which expanded to eight cantons in the mid 14th century, and thirteen cantons between the 16th and 18th centuries. For centuries, this Swiss confederation was little more than a loose alliance aimed at preserving local autonomy with respect to the Empire, without containing any central authority. The cantonal assembly became the form of government of most of the German cantons. Somewhat more ceremonial than the village assembly, the canton meeting could include a parade of the little army of the canton, with the magistrates arriving on horseback amidst banners and horn-blowing. The procedures were slightly less permissive than in the communes. Here, membership was limited to men over the age of 18 or 20 years and proposals had to be previously channeled through the elected council. The assembly voted on cantonal laws and motions, taxes, and admission of new members, and elected canton officials with judicial, police, and other executive functions, as well as the federal deputies. An oath of allegiance to the Constitution was taken from all attendants, including women and children. Fines for nonattendance existed in some cantons.

Continuing into the early 20th century, the size of the cantons' electorate was small, each with a membership between 3,000 and 12,000 men. Their homogeneity is still very high nowadays. Most of the twenty-two cantons created in Switzerland in 1848 have differed more from each other than they do from neighboring countries. Also, the cities developed electoral formulas to appoint a Council and the mayor very early (starting with Freiburg in 1248). Merchants and artisans predominated in these urban settings, especially since the 16th and 17th centuries. Popular assemblies have remained more powerful in rural cantons with small, homogeneous populations. In the late 20th century, the Helvetic Confederation was still mainly an instrument for preserving local popular self-government (Lloyd 1907; Head 1995).

Italian Communes

Throughout the 12th century, the North Italian towns, led by their consuls, became autonomous from the Emperor and the Church authorities. Genoa, Pavia, Pisa, Siena, and many other communes organized themselves around the Assembly of all the citizens, or 'harangue' (*arengo*). They approved the appointment of the Consulate by acclamation, a procedure close to unanimity, or by indirect election. In the second half of the 13th century, the participation of the people expanded. In towns like Genoa and Bologna, regular participants in people's Assemblies numbered between 7,000 and 8,000, which was equivalent to the majority of adult men, or about 15 per cent of the total population (author's calculation with data from Waley 1988: 33ff; Hyde 1973: 115).

In the case of Venice, the election of the doge (duke) by the entire population dates from 697. For almost five hundred years, powerful doges were elected by the Assembly, or harangue, formed by 'a great inclusion of the upper, the middle, the lower, and many other Venetians' (majores, mediocres, minores et magna Ventorum englobatio; Wiel 1895). Since 1172, the people's general Assembly indirectly elected the Great Council (usually attended by about 1,000 to 1,500 men, 30 or more years old), which became the supreme authority, and the Senate.

As the doge's powers were restricted, he ceased to be popularly elected and began to be appointed by the Great Council. In order to do so, the latter adopted an increasingly complicated procedure with up to nine stages of approval ballots and lots which was conceived with the aim of making insincere voting and manipulative strategies unviable. From the 13th to the 15th century, the people's Assembly had to ratify the election of the doge by the Council. Other elected offices, from the 13th century until 1789, included magistrates, procurators, advocates, and a High Chancellor. 'The Republic was founded on the politics of compromise, conciliation, and consensus . . . the patrician Republic gave Venice 500 years of domestic peace and stability' (Finlay 1980, in Lines 1986).

In Florence, republican forms of government, including the election of rulers, existed for more than two hundred years from the late 13th century. During the first republican period, which extended from 1291 to 1433, the people's Assembly was formed by residents over the age of twenty-five who paid some minimum local taxes. This produced Assemblies of more than 6,000 voters, which was equivalent to about 15 per cent of the total number of inhabitants in a city with many youth and immigrants, and certainly included a majority of its adult men (author's calculation with data from Najemy 1982; Brucker 1977: 252, 1983: 133).

The government of Florence was organized around the standard-bearer of justice (*Gonfaloniere*) and the other eight members of the Lordship (*Signoria*). They were elected by a complex system of approval voting and very frequent lots. The *Signoria* was supported by twelve elected advisors or 'good men', sixteen *gonfaloniers* representing the quarters of the city, as well as many other elected offices for which most voters were eligible for short terms (six months or a year). The Council of the People (300 members) and the Council of the Commune (200 members) were selected by a mixed procedure of people's election and appointment by the *Signoria*. As in Venice, albeit with different formulas, an extremely complex procedure of elections was conceived to prevent the fraudulent manipulation of the electoral process and to avert the commune's domination by a few of the city's powerful families. Rulers and officeholders were frequently replaced, and this instituted a certain feeling of apparent instability. Yet a more basic stability was secured by the 'large degree of agreement within the guild community on certain issues, particularly in the economic sphere' (Brucker 1983: 66, 70, 388ff.).

The rule of the Medici, established in 1433, introduced some restrictions and frequent interruptions in the regular schedule of elections. Yet, although some families were disenfranchised, 'new people' were included in the electorate, which, parallel to the growth of the population, reached about 8,000 voters in the late 15th century, again about 15 per cent of total population (according to data in Rubinstein 1966: 214–15). The new republic established in 1494 was based upon the popular election of the traditional offices and of a new Great Council inspired by the Venice model, formed in this case by about 3,000 members. After some decay of the Council's powers, a new period of Medici rule again replaced regular elections with direct approval by people's Assembly. The last Florentine republic re-established the election of the rulers, including the Great Council, from 1527 to 1530 (Brucker 1977, 1983; Guidi 1992).

members participated with commendable frequency in elections whenever the possibilities of such participation were open to them.' The election campaigns were open events, public spectacles, inclusive and popular. Control of elections by local elites became difficult and most elections were open to innovative candidates and uncertain results (O'Gorman 1982: 389ff.).

The active electorate was partly curbed by certain restrictive institutions, most prominently the control of the Parliament by the Cabinet, single-party Cabinets, and the restriction of the political agenda to a few issues on which a homogeneous group could promote some dominant interest. As will be seen in the following section, a series of electoral reforms during the 19th century established more and better defined constituencies across the country, but also more rigid bounds over the groups of citizens entitled to participate in the electoral process than had existed in some of the previous periods (Plumb 1967, 1969; O'Gorman 1982, 1989; Phillips 1982, 1992; Taylor 1997).

Anglo-American Colonies

Elections by virtual universal suffrage in the British colonies in North America date from the election of the House of Burgesses in Virginia in 1619, followed closely by the Assembly of Maryland and the annual choice of governor in Plymouth. In the early part of the history of each colony, the qualifications required of electors were neither numerous nor well-defined, allowing in many cases all inhabitants to vote. Later, suffrage restrictions previously introduced in Britain were extended to the colonies, especially in the form of land-property requirements. In fact, this was not an extemporaneous condition. As with the other European cases already mentioned, the assumption that all family members shared some common basic interest, allowing them to be fairly represented by the head of household, was strongly grounded on the familiy property. In addition, the absence of feudal lords, a much greater availability of land, and the wide diffusion of real and personal property in the North American colonies rendered the British requirements for voting much less restrictive.

Until the independence of the colonies in 1776, large consensus was found in most communities. Unanimity was considered a highly valued goal and conflict over public issues was something to be avoided. In the very earliest times, the right to vote in a colony was claimed in very much the same way as the current right to vote of stockholders in a modern corporation. The early colonies were business corporations in agriculture, hence the real property qualification was considered the appropriate requirement to entitle the holder to a vote. The assumption was that suffrage was the way to identify the common good of the community and only those who clearly had an interest in the colony should be permitted to participate in its governance (Porter 1969; Dinkin 1977).

The requirements for voting rights were loosely defined and differed in every colony. They were adapted to different circumstances in order to make feasible the identification of common interests among the voters and the stability of the social choice. The rules were flexible and were frequently modified, using either land property, wealth, or moral qualifications as indices of the individual's capability to make reasonable choices on collective matters.

More specifically, those who had not been residents a sufficient length of time were excluded from voting. But the length of time required varied from six months to one or two years, depending on the colony, and did not exist in Virginia, New Hampshire, and New York. The standard minimum age requirement was 21 years old (20 in Plymouth, 18 in Rhode Island). Yet 'minors did sometimes vote' (Bishop 1893: 65); 'boys and other [legally] unqualified persons voted' in the Carolinas (Seymour and Frary 1918, vol. 1: 223); 'boys' and 'youth' 18 and 19 years old participated in certain elections in North Carolina, Pennsylvania, New Hampshire, and Massachusetts. All women could vote in New Jersey (Dinkin, 1977: 30–1). Other voting criteria included the character of the man's employment and his moral qualifications. Land-property was measured in acres in the South, but in New England, where land was more expensive, much smaller portions were validated for its monetary value.

On the one hand, criminals were disenfranchised and, in several Northern colonies, the absence of correctness in moral behavior could lead to the suppression of a freeman's rights and even to his total disenfranchisement, in some cases making resource of the testimony of his neighbors. In Massachusetts and New York, electors were required to be members of some church; Roman Catholics in general, and Jews and Quakers in some cases, could not vote. On the other hand, in the Southern colonies, where the majority of the black, red (or native), and mulatto population resided, they voted until rather late (1716 in South Carolina, 1734 in North Carolina, 1723 in Virginia, 1761 in Georgia). In the North, no state ever eliminated nonwhites from the ballot, including Indians in parts of New England.

A number of historians have found the franchise to have been extremely widespread despite the qualifications imposed upon prospective electors. 'Fairly uniformly the electorate seems to have varied, on a freehold basis exclusively, from about 50 to 75 per cent [of the male adult population]. Some communities exceeded, some fell below this range, but probably not as many as came within its limits' (Williamson 1960: 38). 'In some colonies like Virginia the degree of eligibility may have run as high as 80 per cent, in others, such as New York, it was closer to 50 or 60 per cent.' In general, enfranchisement was larger in rural districts. According to some sources of the 1770s, qualifications were rarely scrutinized: 'anything with the appearance of a man' was allowed to vote. Actually, only 'one-fifth to one-half of the adult males' were unable to exercise the right to vote (Dinkin 1977: 41–9). Accordingly, and quite similarly to other continental European cases previously discussed, between 10 and 20 per cent of the total population seem to have had voting rights in the British colonies in North America before their independence.

In colonial times, the annual election day was a gala event, conceived as an occasion for the colonists to come together and socialize. Procedures included oral voting, show of hands, polls, a booth with a poll-book with the names of the candidates over and against which were set down the votes, or corn and bean ballots to approve or reject the candidates for certain offices. Written ballots have been used in some places since the early 17th century, and some forms of the modern perforated ballot with the names of all the candidates were used from the late 17th century.

The elections of local representatives were instrumental in the process towards independence. Yet, between 1776 and the approval of the Constitution of the United States in 1789, a tendency towards higher uniformity developed across the states. Wishing to preserve harmony in a larger, more varied society, most patriot leaders thought that political participation should be preserved for those who had a 'common interest with, and an attachment to the community', those with a 'stake in society', for they alone could make competent, reasonable judgements.

Interestingly, a new strategy of simultaneous enfranchisement and disenfranchisement of different electors' groups, which would be steadily developed throughout the 19th century, can be identified as early as in the independence years. On the one hand, property requirements were reduced and became similar in all thirteen states, religious requirements were substantially moderated so as to make almost all Christians eligible, and several states allowed blacks to possess the franchise for the first time. Yet, on the other hand, formal requirements of 21 years of age, male gender, citizenship, and residence were established in all states, and eight states altered their own constitutions in order to exclude blacks, slaves, and most Indians from voting. All in all, the electorate of the 13 states 'probably expanded from 50–80 per cent [of the male adult population] in the late provincial period to about 60–90 per cent by the close of the revolutionary period' (Dinkin 1982), which is to say about 15–25 per cent of the total population.

Iberian-American Colonies

Universal men's suffrage at the local level was introduced into the Spanish colonies in North and South America more abruptly than in the British colonies. Following the Napoleonic invasion of Spain in 1808, an improvised people's resistance was coordinated by means of elected local *juntas*, which initially adopted the rules of the surviving medieval Assemblies (*Cortes*) and local councils. In 1809, representatives of the Central Junta of Spain were indirectly elected with restricted suffrage by municipal and parish councils using a mix of choices and lots.

The election of new 'Cortes' in 1810 and 1812 was based on a combination of old rules and the new suffrage of family heads. The 1812 Constitution approved in Cádiz introduced virtual male universal suffrage for indirect elections, as was used for the elections of municipal councils and provincial deputies in 1812–14. Paralleling the enlargement of the electorate, the proportion of representatives from the Spanish colonies in the Americas and the Philippines was augmented. In 1812, all men aged over 25, and natives of the province, whatever their status, could vote. Exclusions were devised for some groups on the basis of the presumption that they did not share some basic common interest with the rest of the community. Among those excluded were the members of the military orders, state debtors, servants, and those lacking employment, a trade, or any other 'honest livelihood'. Native Indians in the colonies, however, were allowed to vote (Chavarri 1988; Demélas-Bohy and Guerra 1996).

This initial electoral mobilization, which was soon interrupted in Spain with the re-establishment of the traditional monarchy, was a major episode in the Spanish colonies' process of gaining independence. More than one hundred American cities were involved in the first Spanish elections and electoral politics mobilized large groups in the immediate aftermath. The fall of Spanish domination fostered territorial fragmentation and localism. Electoral expectations were concentrated at the first electoral level, including rural towns, small cities, and provincial states (Botana 1995). This push explains the 'early existence [in 1820] of a relatively wide suffrage in the Spanish world . . . With a few exceptions, in most Latin American countries the idea of an extended suffrage gained ground during the first half of the 19th century to an extent which has few parallels in the Western World' (Posada-Carbó 1996: 6).

Particularly interesting developments include those in New Spain (today's Mexico) in 1812–20. For the election of representatives to both the Spanish *Cortes* and local and provincial councils, electoral districts were defined as corresponding to the traditional parishes, which were socially somewhat homogeneous units. In many places the Indian Republics were transformed into town councils. The Indians were thus given access to the election and the holding of all the offices, while maintaining the homogeneity of every electoral unit. In this way, voting practices enjoyed large consensus within the communities. In 1814, voting rights were given to all adult men 18 years old or younger if married, including not only all Indians but also 'patriotic foreigners' (Annino 1995, 1996).

Similarly, the province of Buenos Aires, as well as other provinces in Rio de la Plata (today's Argentina), organized elections with flexible rules in 1811. More formally, universal suffrage for direct elections of representatives was established for all men more than 20 years old in 1821. Foreigners were excluded, but voting rights were given to about 20 per cent of the total population (Chiaramonte 1995; Alonso 1996).

The Crown of Portugal called elections in 1821, according to the rules provided by the Spanish Constitution of 1812. In Brazil, 'the elections mobilized the interest of the majority of the male adult population of the towns. There were no restrictions of race or literacy'. Economic requisites were low and could be fulfilled by all 'except beggars and vagabunds [sic]', and slaves. Elections were lively, popular events with relatively wide participation. 'Approximately, a half of free men 24 years old or more were in the census and, in some provinces, the number rose to 85 per cent' (Graham 1995).

Political mobilization was curbed and voting rights were substantially reduced in the second half of the 19th century in most of the new states in Iberian America as well as in Spain and Portugal. Relatively small, homogeneous communities were, thus, able to make important collective decisions on the basis of elections with broad voting rights. But the sudden creation of new large states with wide franchise produced greater political instability.

2.2. COMPLEX ELECTORATES

The complexity of large electorates in modern polities derives from new demands of public goods and new policy issues that are submitted to binding collective decisions by voting. The more the number of issues in the political agenda and the dispersion of the corresponding voters' preferences increase, the more uncertain the social choice becomes. Stable and satisfactory outcomes can be obtained only with the introduction of new institutional devices.

The introduction of new voters into the electorate can be considered to be either innocuous, hazardous, or threatening, from the point of view of the incumbent voters and rulers, depending on the number of new voters, their political information, the 'location' of their preferences, and the degree of homogeneity of their interests, as well as on the fragmentation of the incumbents. Specifically, dependent people with preferences similar to the incumbent voters, like children, youth, women, and servants, can be considered innocuous or susceptible to being manipulated in order to enlarge the support of incumbents' preferences and even to counteract the potential threat derived from the enfranchisement of other groups of voters. In contrast, other politically unorganized and uninformed new voters, especially those in rural areas, can produce less predictable social choices because of persuasion by intrepid political entrepreneurs. Finally, colonized peoples, dominated ethnic groups, or compact working classes, if allowed to vote, are often expected to threaten the survival of existing states, property rights, and moral standards and to reverse the previous political equilibrium.

Incumbent rulers, especially if they have a high degree of internal cohesion and face weak opposition movements, tend to prefer reduced electorates and restrictive electoral systems producing total winners and total losers, as was the case with most incumbent Conservatives and Liberals in the 19th century. Emergent minorities, in contrast, tend to pressure for the enlargement of the electorate and, at the same time, for proportional representation or other pluralistic institutional formulas, as the Socialists did in many countries in the late 19th century.

However, if the incumbent rulers are submitted to a sufficiently credible challenge, they may prefer to lead the enlargement of the electorate in conjunction with the introduction of pluralistic institutions which guarantee them some power-sharing, as certain Conservatives did in the late 19th century and early 20th century. Conversely, the challenging opposition may bet for universal suffrage, but also for maintaining simple institutional formulas, including, in particular, single-member electoral districts, in the expectation of becoming absolute winners under the existing framework.

This section has two parts. First, arguments for and against the enlargement of the electorate are reviewed. Second, different strategies of voting rights are identified on the basis of different combinations of enfranchisement of new voters' groups and institutional arrangements.

Arguments on Suffrage

Arguments for and against the extension of suffrage rights became more controversial and sophisticated in modern times, as new, large political units encompassed potentially complex electorates, than those of the earlier, local-type discussed in the previous section. The development of communications and travel, bigger markets, larger-scale economies, division of labor, and other factors supporting the creation of modern nation-states, make political communities more complex and the allocation of voting rights more intricate.

Traditional doctrines of permanent, natural rights have been widely used in favor of the enlargement of the electorate. On this view, equal voting rights are defended on the assumption that all human beings are created equal. Yet this assumption may suggest a substantial degree of harmony and homogeneous interests among the potential members of a political community, which is relatively hard to find in modern societies. A logical evolution of the natural rights argument has led some of its believers to emphasize certain supposedly common social and cultural characteristics of human nature, actually making the requirements for the corresponding voting rights more restrictive. At the same time, collective natural rights have been argued in order to maintain traditional estates' 'organic' representation or the privileges of incumbent voters.

Partly as a result of these theoretical weaknesses among early promoters of broad-based suffrage, alternative arguments more clearly based on the expected consequences of enlarging the existing electorates have tended to replace the natural rights argument, especially on the side of those against creating new voting rights. In fact, hardly any social group has been indisputably recognized to bear natural voting rights and most have been excluded, or at least proposed to be excluded, at some moment or place for a variety of reasons.

Children, aliens, the mentally ill, criminals, and the homeless are almost always barred from voting, on the assumption that they are unable to make reasonable choices on collective matters or that they do not share sufficiently significant common interests with the other members of the community. Analogously, women were traditionally considered to be insufficiently involved in public affairs to participate in political elections; many youth and children are still considered too immature to make political choices; the elderly have been seen as particularly vulnerable to manipulation due to their dependence on state pensions; Indians, blacks, and Jews have been considered extraneous to the interests of incumbent dominant voters; and industrial workers have been widely viewed as a threatening majority which should be prevented becoming an electoral force.

Conversely, but also on the basis of expected political consequences, landowners, monarchists, and Catholics were threatened with deprivation or effectively deprived of voting rights by modern liberal movements because of their allegiance to the old regime. Attempts to exclude peasants from voting were based on their servile obedience to the owners. Artisans, shopkeepers, and other 'bourgeois' people were attacked for their social dominance in some industrialized settings with a growing proletariat.

In all these different arguments, the crucial social choice variable is the dispersion of voters' preferences, that is, the number of new potential voters and the 'location' of their preferences relative to the number and preferences of the incumbent voters. When the enfranchisable group is presumed to have very similar or interlaced preferences as the incumbent voters, no significant change in the social choice can be predicted from its enfranchisement. When new voters' preferences are uncertain and one suspects that they will make hesitant, shifting choices, the room for manipulation of the social choice is great and the outcome appears to be unpredictable and unstable. When new voters have compact, differentiated preferences and can form an alternative majority, they may produce a new social choice which can be considered very damaging for the incumbent voters or, from the opposite viewpoint but coincidental analysis, very satisfactory for the newly enfranchised. The arguments that correspond to these analyses are reviewed below. (For a comparable threefold typology of rhetorical arguments regarding civic liberties, universal suffrage, and social policy, see Hirschman 1991.)

Innocuousness

Certain authors have held that 'dependent' people, as they are led by those who are active in politics and share the same interests, are not likely to develop differentiated political preferences. Children, youth, women, servants, serfs, and slaves have been considered to have the same stake in the society as those already enfranchised.

The idea of virtual representation emerged in rather homogeneous societies during the Middle Ages. At that time it was believed that, like the father of a traditional household could vote on behalf of his wife and children, paternalistic rulers could act on behalf of those under their care. When adapted to modern times, this argument was based upon the presumption that nonvoters did not bear a potential distortion of the social choice, but were unnecessary participants in a process in which they would vote like the members of the incumbent winning group.

The concept of virtual representation without voting was used as an argument against the enfranchisement of the colonists, in particular in the British colonies in North America. During the controversy that led to the war for American independence, certain British politicians asserted that the House of Commons did in fact represent the colonists, even if they did not elect their own representatives to the House, because they shared the same interests as those voting in Britain.

As a consistent reply to these statements, the independence of the colonies was supported by the argument that the Americans had become 'a different people', that is, that they had ceased to have preferences similar to and amalgamated with those of the Britons and had developed differentiated interests and new issues, which were not sufficiently dealt with in the House of Commons. However, this did not prevent the independent American communities from using similar arguments in order to keep certain people disenfranchised or to add other groups to those already banned from voting, including women and children, under the presumption that they did not have different interests from those of the enfranchised male adults.

The English liberal James Mill drew from this discussion the implication that certain dependent groups in the society were not worth being given new voting rights. Mill supported significant enlargements of the electorate in Britain in the early 19th century, but he stopped short of including 'superfluous' voters. In a series of articles published between 1820 and 1829, just before the first British electoral reform in 1832, Mill emphasized the leading role of the 'middle class' in promoting stability and prosperity for the whole society, in the same way the 'median voter' has been considered able to produce high social utility in modern social choice theory. Specifically, Mill hoped to curb the role of the minority aristocracy in order to promote liberal reforms. He also counted on the fact that a vast majority of people feeling an immediate and daily dependence (through jobs, income, protection, housing, and health) upon the members of the middle class 'would be sure to be guided by their advise and example'.

Accordingly, James Mill was in favor of a broad men's suffrage including 'certain classes, professions, or fraternities' that had become central in modern society but had been excluded from voting during the previous period. Yet, he thought that any other portion of the community beyond these groups, 'if erected into the choosing body, would remain the same'. The logical inference for Mill was to recommend a virtual men's suffrage, while noting that 'all those individuals whose interests are indisputably included in those of other individuals, may be struck off [the electorate] without inconvenience'. These included, in particular, all children and youth whose interests are involved in those of their parents. James Mill expected that, since the great majority of old men had children, whose interests they regarded as an essential part of their own, even without voting the interests of the young would not be sacrificed to those of the old. Likewise, he considered that voting rights could be fairly denied to women since 'the interest of almost [*sic*] all of whom is involved either in that of their fathers or in that of their husbands' (Mill, 1820–9, in Lively and Rees 1978).

Interestingly, this point was eventually recycled by the suffragist movement as the basis for the harmlessness of giving voting rights to women. 'If the opinions and interests of women are identical with those of men of a similar social grade', said the American suffragist Lydia E. Becker, 'there could be no possible harm in giving them the same means of expressing them as are given to men' (Becker 1872).

In further developments, the expectation that women would reveal the same political preferences as their previously enfranchised fathers and husbands led some political leaders to perceive women's suffrage as an opportunity to counteract the innovative influence of other newly enfranchised groups with more differentiated preferences, including workers, immigrants, and blacks. The American suffragist Mary Putnam Jacobi, in particular, developed this 'counter-weight' argument. She praised women's values in favor of 'conservatism, their economy, their horror of waste, their interest in personal character, the very simplicity of their judgement, their preoccupation with direct and living issues, all qualities generated by the special circumstances which have surrounded women, and must continue to surround them', as reasons for giving them the vote. Jacobi expected that 'the influence of the women who are now busily engaged in civilizing the hordes of uncivilized people in our midst, will be utilized, not only to kindle the lagging interest of the men of their own class, but to so guide ignorant women voters, that they could be made to counterbalance, when necessary, the votes of ignorant and interested men' (Jacobi 1894).

With a similar orientation, Catholic and conservative women created the French Union for Women's Suffrage, the first specifically suffragist national organization in France, in 1909. They equated women's emancipation to the defense of the Church, the family, and the fatherland. More specifically, they promoted a formula of 'family suffrage' by which only the head of the family would vote, but with as many votes as there were members of the family, including women, grandparents, and children, in the assumption that all of them shared the same interests (Rosanvallon 1992).

The 'innocuousness' argument became more sophisticated as the suffragist movement proceeded. As the traditional sphere of women in the household was becoming more public through the development of food stores, laundry operators, and public schools, as well as more women entering the labor market, it was argued that their basic interests merged with those of the incumbent male voters in two different ways. First, these changes provoked new family relationships, making men's tasks closer to certain traditional women's household jobs. Second, women began to share similar professional and economic interests with their male counterparts (Kraditor 1965, esp. ch. 3; Harvey 1998).

Hazard

Paralleling the self-confident argument of innocuousness, there is an age-old tradition that points to the risks of permitting the electoral participation of ignorant people who are likely to be deceived in their political choices. As the 'hazard' argument was formulated, for instance, in a mid 18th century French local assembly regarding the election of artisans as deputies, certain people can be considered 'easy to delude, incapable of understanding by themselves what might be in the town's interests, and sometimes unable to write the name of those for whom they were voting' (Temple 1973: 78).

Lack of political understanding has typically been considered to be the result of illiteracy, which may prevent an individual from even recognizing the names of candidates. This argument has taken precedence in countries in which a sudden enlargement of the electorate has been introduced or proposed in an environment of massive illiteracy and the absence of sufficiently well-organized political parties, including those in many 19th-century European states. To the alarmed observer, misinformed voters could be the victims of patrons, would-be dictators, demagogues, fanatics, or extremists of varied colors. Then the social choice would be unpredictable and unstable since shifting majorities could be formed at the initiative of ambitious leaders. Suffrage rights were typically seen in this perspective as a 'slippery slope' leading to the unknown.

This type of warning was issued against the 'innocuousness' argument mentioned earlier, and was developed by Chancellor Otto Fürst von Bismarck when he promoted universal male suffrage in the North German Confederation (and later in the German Empire). He implicitly expected that peasants, who were loyal to the King overall, would also be obedient to their manor lords or employers when voting (Ludwig 1927: 242). Yet, as was pointed out by the lawyer Robert von Mohl, certain potential political entrepreneurs who had been previously marginalized from the political, such as the Catholic clergy in the rural areas and the Socialist or Communist leaders in factories and mines, might take control of new voters and produce a high fractionalization of the elected representatives. 'Universal manhood suffrage, without firmly established and well organized political parties', he warned, 'especially in a federated state like Germany, would bring forth numerous fractions incapable of forming a majority—a parliament built upon quicksand' (Mohl 1860–9, in Anderson and Anderson 1967: 427).

This position could also be found on the left wing of the political spectrum. In situations in which large sections of the population were deprived of voting in political elections, a number of Liberal, Radical, and Socialist leaders were reluctant about significant enlargements of the electorate. They feared that uninformed new voters would be deceived by unscrupulous political entrepreneurs or by their own bosses and patrons. Instead of focusing on voting rights, many political leaders of the left gave priority to promoting public education and compulsory schooling, which was considered to be a tool for building a better society and, more specifically, a necessary condition for shaping more 'conscious', homogeneous constituencies that would support progressive programs.

The British Socialist Robert Owen, for example, did not refrain from referring to 'the ignorance, vulgarity, and most disgusting assumptions of the laboring classes' and, accordingly, considered that a government based upon popular elections 'could be tolerated only as the best known means of leading to an advanced state of society, by a superior education of all classes' (Owen 1828, 1844, in 1993, vol. 1: liii; vol. 2: 121).

When universal male suffrage was introduced in France in 1848, the Socialist Pierre-Joseph Proudhon held that 'universal suffrage given to a people of so neglected an education as ours, far from being the instrument of progress, is only the stumbling-block of liberty' (Proudhon 1923, vol. XVII: t. 1). On the same occasion, the Socialist Louis Blanc asked to adjourn the elections in order to prevent 'the numerical superiority of the ignorant peasantry over the enlightened population of the towns' (Blanc 1848: 297). Likewise, the revolutionary Louis-Auguste Blanqui referred to the oppressed workers as a 'blind flock', due to their control by the Church, and announced that 'the elections, if they are held, will be reactionary' (Bastid 1948).

In Italy, the proposal to abolish literacy tests for allocating voting rights in a largely illiterate population was viewed as running the risk of having the rural masses of the South being politically manipulated by traditional local powerholders. This was particularly risky for national cohesion in such an early period of unification of the Italian state. Meanwhile, in Spain certain 19th-century Liberals rejected universal male suffrage in the fear that new, uneducated voters would be deceived by their patrons, *caudillos*, and local bosses (*caciques*). In the face of that risk, the progressive Sabino Herrero stated: 'It is better to delay universal suffrage rather than falsify it' (Serrano 1993: 215–16).

Regarding women's suffrage in particular, certain Liberal leaders in European countries feared that women would be manipulated by the Church and would submit to reactionary influence. This was a reaction to the conservative 'counter-weight' arguments for women's suffrage previously described. The British Liberal William E. Gladstone held that women's 'personal attendance' at elections would constitute a 'practical evil not only of the gravest, but even of an intolerable character' (Lewis 1987: 67). The Radical French Prime Minister Georges Clemenceau believed that 'if the right to vote were given to women tomorrow, France would all of a sudden jump backwards into the middle ages' (Hause 1984: 16).

According to some Socialist leaders of the early 20th century, women's voting rights should be subordinated to their economic liberation, which implied the abolition of private property. Only by suppressing the existing family relations supported by a capitalist economy, they thought, would gender equality come about as a natural consequence, while, under capitalism, women's vote would be somewhat adrift from the point of view of progressive purposes. The French and Belgian Socialists voted for a long time against women's suffrage, fearing the more conservative preferences of women and their domination by the priests.

As late as 1931, most Spanish left-wing Republicans opposed the introduction of female suffrage into the newly established Second Republic on the grounds that the new voters would be won over by the conservative clergy. The opposition included two outspoken Radical-Socialist and Socialist female politicians (the latter in disagreement with most of her male party companions), Victoria Kent and Margarita Nelken, respectively. Kent, in particular, confined women's voting rights to their achievement of a 'university education and the liberation of their consciousness' (Capel 1992).

Threat

In contrast to the presumptions that nonvoters would be either innocuous or easily manipulated, they can also be seen as threatening by incumbent voters when they share some compact common preference which is opposed to the prevailing rule, especially regarding property or moral standards. A new majority entering the electorate can change the social choice dramatically at the expense of the previous winners. In early modern periods of enlargement of voting rights, this foresight was simultaneously

unavoidable and irreducible Communism'. In 1888, facing a new attempt to introduce broad suffrage in Spain, he noted a difference between the hazard of voting by illiterates and the threat of voting by the poor. 'I believe', he said, 'that universal suffrage, if it is sincere, if it gives a real vote in the governance of the country to the crowd, not only the unlearned, which would be almost irrelevant, but to the miserly and beggar mob, it would be the triumph of Communism and the ruin of the principle of property' (Cánovas 1884–90).

Interestingly, the prospect that alternative winners could develop under the opportunities created by broad adult suffrage and reverse the basis of the existing social structures was also confirmed by the opposing side. For most Socialists, the experience of universal suffrage in France in 1848, which led to the direct election of Louis Bonaparte as President of the Republic and eventually to the dissolution of the Assembly by coup and the re-establishment of the Empire, was extremely disappointing. This episode made most of them highly suspicious of such mechanisms of social choice and, as mentioned, led them to put their trust, instead, in the long-term effects of public education or, more generally, in the guidance of educated leaders. In one of its branches, this Socialist approach supported the role of intellectuals leading the ignorant working masses in the formation of workers' political parties, which inspired both the formation of Socialist parties under Karl Kautsky's leadership and the organization of the 'revolutionary vanguard' in Communist parties by Vladimir Lenin.

However, some ambiguity remained, which permitted the development of the alternative opinion in favor of universal suffrage as an opportunity for a new majority to be formed. As early as 1852, Karl Marx had written that, in contrast to what was happening in France, 'universal suffrage [would be] the equivalent of political power for the working class in England, where the proletariat forms the large majority of the population', confirming thus the implicit 'threat' that defenders of private ownership had perceived in workers' votes. Marx speculated that 'the carrying of universal suffrage in England would be a far more socialistic measure than anything which has been honored with that name on the Continent. Its inevitable result, here [in the United Kingdom], would be the political supremacy of the working class' (Marx 1852: 332).

After the introduction of virtual universal men's suffrage in Germany, Marx noted in 1880 that 'the franchise has been transformed from a means of deception, which it was before, into an instrument of emancipation'. Further developing this insight, Friedrich Engels sketched a potentially winning coalition under universal suffrage elections starting with 'the most numerous, most compact mass, the decisive "shock force" of the international proletarian army' that would 'conquer the greater part of the middle strata of society, petty [sic] bourgeois and small peasants, and grow into the decisive power of the land, before which all other powers will have to bow, whether they like it or not' (Engels 1895: 421). This approach was further elaborated by Edward Bernstein in the early 20th century and eventually became the basis for the electoral participation of the Social-Democrats.

Analogously, the expectation that not only workers' but also women's political rights could bring about substantial changes in certain social structures and moral standards was not only feared by certain men, as previously mentioned, but sustained by some outstanding leaders of the feminist movement. In the early days of the movement, Mary Wollstonecraft had outlined this idea. She openly acknowledged that the existing ignorance of women generated their 'folly'. But she argued for women's rights in the expectation of obtaining beneficial social consequences, specifically 'the moral improvement that a revolution in female manners might naturally be expected to produce' in the dominating men's society (Wollstonecraft 1792, ch. 13).

Just as anti-feminists held that social order required a family model that involved the political subordination of women, some radical suffragists hoped that women's political rights would produce significant changes in family relations. Women's political participation would give salience to new issues related to education, social welfare, and children and, as a consequence, public life would be morally elevated. Governments based on women's suffrage would even be 'less likely to go to war, without real necessity', as stated in the American Congressional Union for Woman Suffrage (Kraditor 1965: 63).

These arguments were also developed by some outstanding male supporters of women's voting rights, such as John Stuart Mill, one of the founders of the British women's suffrage movement. On the one hand, Mill shared the worries of other progressive leaders previously mentioned regarding the votes of uneducated people. 'Universal teaching must precede universal enfranchisement', he said. Mill even supported giving different numbers of votes to different individuals on the basis of their respective educations (Mill 1861, ch. 8). Yet, on the other hand, if women were educated and enfranchised in all aspects of life, Mill thought, they would make a substantial contribution to public life on the basis of their distinctive intellectual and moral qualities. With women's political participation, 'all the selfish propensities, the self-worship, the unjust self-preference, which exist among mankind would be permanently rooted out'. Women's influence would be 'nothing but favorable to public virtue' (Mill 1869, ch. 4).

Susan B. Anthony, the foremost agitator for women's suffrage in the United States in the 19th century, argued more specifically that the prevalence of such social plagues as prostitution, sex crimes, and wife murders proved men's incapacity to cope with social problems, that they were caused by women's dependence, and that their cure would be women's economic independence and political equality. 'I am a full and firm believer', she said, 'in the revelation that it is through women that the [human] race is to be redeemed. And it is because of this faith that I ask for her immediate and unconditional emancipation from all political, industrial, social and religious subjection' (Anthony 1875).

Similarly, the leader of the French suffragists, Hubertine Auclert, claimed that women's political liberation would reduce war, immorality, and alcoholism and would create the opportunity for building a 'maternal State' in charge of public health care, and the protection of children, ill people, the unemployed, and the elderly (Auclert 1885, in Hause, 1987).

Voting Rights Strategies

As has been seen, natural rights arguments regarding the enlargement of the electorate were largely replaced with social-utility arguments in the modern intellectual debate. For some of the authors and politicians mentioned, voting rights were openly acknowledged to be a means for the goal of social utility. For others, the argument of social utility was adopted only as a means for persuading reluctant incumbent rulers and voters of the advantages of 'natural' equal suffrage. In the latter approach, the expediency argument was itself an expedient, but in some ways it also induced its bearers to pay attention to the collective consequences of individuals' voting rights.

In some cases, universal suffrage has been established in modern times in parallel with a decrease in the dispersion of preferences among different social groups on certain relevant issues. Certainly, universal suffrage can produce widely satisfactory and stable outcomes, while becoming itself a stable feature in the polity, on the basis of certain voters' characteristics, such as high educational levels, significant opportunities for economic well-being, and low barriers between different ethnic and gender groups. Yet, certain institutional arrangements can attain similar objectives, either by reducing the number of the available alternatives at voting, or by transferring the social choice to a post-electoral, institutional stage of moderating negotiations in a pluralistic framework.

Among the authors and politicians previously discussed, some wanted to exclude those without property from voting in order to preserve the existing social equilibrium. Others pointed to the socially efficient potential role of the 'middle class', but they only conceived this by way of obtaining adhesion from other groups to the middle group's interests through some 'enlightened' or 'sound' judgement. Others, finally, sought to establish the supremacy of the 'working class', but relied upon 'the conquest' of the middle strata of society.

All these strategies were aimed at maintaining or creating a single absolute majority in favor of one group's interests. They had in common the assumption that the act of voting can immediately produce a social choice. But further institutional refinements in the process of decision making, including in particular proportional representation, were able to create a different framework. Even if each member of a group votes according to some differentiated group's interest, further multiparty bargaining and compromising within a pluralistic institutional setting can produce intermediate, moderate, 'middle', 'enlightened', or 'sound' social choices able to distribute social utility widely and evenly. This was a relatively late discovery. Accordingly, different choices of institutions have paralleled different strategies of voting rights in various countries on the basis of the social choices they can be expected to produce.

From the point of view of incumbent voters and leaders, a successful strategy of voting rights allocation should achieve two major aims. First, it should keep within safe limits the instability effects of new, uneducated voters prone to shift their choices with successive elections or, in the words introduced earlier, to limit the 'hazards' of enlarged franchise. Second, it should prevent the formation of an alternative electoral majority able to change existing social structures and moral standards radically, or to neutralize the 'threat' posed by new voters. As suggested before, 'innocuous' voters—those likely to duplicate the voting patterns of the incumbents, as it was widely expected that would be the case, in particular, with women's enfranchisement—can be used by incumbent leaders to enlarge the electoral support of prevailing positions and to neutralize the influence of other newly enfranchised voters with hazardous or threatening preferences.

Two basic institutional elements can be manipulated in order to achieve these aims: (1) legal requirements for access to voting rights; (2) institutional regulations that can shape the party system, particularly the electoral rules.

On the basis of different combinations of these and related elements, three basic strategies of voting rights can be identified in the history of the early processes of democratization. The first, the 'Anglo' model, is based on a gradual allocation of voting rights to different minority groups through a slow, lengthy process of moderate reforms while the available political alternatives are reduced to a two-party system by institutional means. In this way, each small step in the enfranchisement of a new minority group forces its members to enter into collaboration with one of the two existing larger parties, thus giving the incumbents the possibility of maintaining significant control of the political agenda and retaining some winning positions. The result of this process, which refers to the cases of the United Kingdom, the United States, and other ex-British colonies, brings about high stability in the long term, but also some significant institutional restrictions over the development of varied political preferences, as well as relatively low levels of political participation.

The second strategy, the 'Latin' model, involves a sudden jump from a small electorate to universal men's suffrage, typically at the initiative of the political left or new groups, and under single-winner electoral rules. In conditions of mass illiteracy and the absence of well-organized political parties, as was the case at the moment of introducing broad suffrage rights for first time in France, Italy, Spain, as well as in some 'Latin' colonies in the Americas and Africa, this strategy tends to provoke high electoral unpredictability and instability, often leading to conflict and nondemocratic comebacks.

Finally, the third, the 'Nordic' model, which was developed in Germany and in Northern European countries, such as Sweden, Norway, and Finland, makes the sudden enfranchisement of a very large electorate compatible with appreciable degrees of political stability. In order to achieve this, new institutional devices in favor of political pluralism are introduced 'from above' by the incumbent rulers. In particular, proportional representation or similar institutional 'safeguards' promoting multiparty politics are adopted. Governments can then rely upon parliamentary coalitions in which centrist and moderate parties can expect to play a decisive role. In this way, the risk of instability and the threat of turnabouts are limited, and incumbent voters and leaders can expect continued opportunities of being included in government and maintaining a significant influence on the political process. As a consequence of self-reinforcing multiparty strategies, the new pluralistic institutional arrangements tend to last.

Tables 2.1, 2.2, and 2.3 show different stages in the process of enlarging voting rights in several countries. The size of the electorate is given as the percentage of enfranchised voters out of total population. The relative increase (or decrease) at each step (presented in the far right column) shows that the United Kingdom, the United States, as well as the former British colonies, Canada, Australia, and New Zealand, have developed a pattern of successive moderate enlargements, never enlarging the existing electorate by more than a few percentage points of the total population, and in two-digit points for women's suffrage only. The smoothness of this path has been reinforced by additional devices that distort representation in favor of traditional incumbent voters or that discourage electoral participation.

In contrast, both the Latin group formed by France, Italy, and Spain, and the Nordic group formed by Germany, Sweden, Norway, and Finland have

TABLE 2.1. *Size of the electorate: The 'Anglo' model*

Country	Voting rights requirements	Electors as % of total population	Percentage points increase
United Kingdom			
1716–1831	Loose rules	3	
1832–1866	Adult (age 21) men, with tax	4	+1
1867–1884	Adult men, with lower tax	8–9	+4
1885–1917	Adult men, with even lower tax	15–19	+6
1918–1927	Adult men, some women	44–49	+25
1928–1970	Adult men and women	65–70	+16
1971–	Men and women (age 18)	72–78	+2
United States			
1776–1788	Loose rules	15	
1789–1878	Adult (age 21) white men, property or tax	16–20	+1
1879–1919	Adult white, non-southern black men	21–24	+1
1919–1963	Plus adult women	49–55	+25
1964–1970	Plus southern blacks	60	+5
1971–	Men and women (age 18)	67–70	+7
Canada			
1891–1917	European adult (age 21) men	25–30	
1918–1959	European adult men and women	50–55	+20
1960–1970	Plus Indians and Innuit	55–60	
1971–	Men and women (age 18)	60–65	
Australia			
1901–1902	Adult (age 21) men, with tax, some women	25	
1902–1967	Adult men and women, except Aboriginals	50–55	+25
1968–1972	Adult men and women	55	
1973–	Men and women (age 18)	60–65	+5
New Zealand			
1851–1875	European adult (age 21) men, property or rent	15	
1876–1892	Adult men	25–30	+10
1893–1964	Adult men and women	48–55	+18
1965–1973	Younger (age 20) men and women	55	
1974–	Men and women (age 18)	60–65	+5

Note: Value ranges regarding total population are due to demographic changes.

Source: Author's own calculations with data from Mackie and Rose (1991) and Mitchell (1992–5).

experienced dramatic increases of the electorate. In all cases, the introduction of male adult suffrage implied that the previous number of voters was multiplied in a single move and that the new voters were a two-digit percentage of the total population. Yet, while in the mentioned Latin-European countries early sudden enlargements of the electorate produced conflictive, short-lived, or fake experiences of virtual universal male suffrage, in their Northern European counterparts a more institutionalized framework allowed pluralistic democracy to last for a number of decades.

Figure 2.1 compares the paths of two extreme cases that experienced

TABLE 2.2. *Size of the electorate: The 'Latin' model*

Country	Voting rights requirements	Electors as % of total population	Percentage points in increase
France			
1791–1795	Adult (age 25) male family heads, with tax	15	
1801–1814	Adult (age 21) men	20	+5
1815–1847	Adult men, with tax	1	–19
1848–1851	Adult men	27	+26
....			
1871–1936	Adult men	20–29	
....			
1945–1972	Adult men and women	63–57	
1973–	Men and women (age 18)	65	+8
Italy			
1861–1881	Adult (age 25) men, with property, tax, literacy	2	
1882–1911	Adult (age 21) men, with tax, literacy	7	+5
1912–1918	Adult (age 21) men with literacy or draft (age 30)	28	+23
1919	Adult men	32	+4
....			
1946–1974	Adult men and women	64–68	
1975–	Men and women (age 18)	78	+10
Spain			
1810,20,36	Adult (age 25) male family heads	28–33	
....			
1834–1867	Adult men, with tax	1–4	
1868–1875	Adult men	25–29	+21
1876–1889	Adult men, with tax	5	–24
1890–1923	Adult men	23–25	+20
....			
1931–1932	Adult men	26	
1933–1936	Adult men and women	53–55	+27
....			
1977–1978	Adult men and women	70	
1979–	Men and women (age 18)	77–80	+7

Note and *Sources*: As for Table 2.1. Dotted lines indicate authoritarian periods.

stable results: the United States with its long, gradual process of enlargement of the electorate, and Sweden with its sudden, dramatic mass enfranchisement.

Cases: Creating Complex Electorates

The three voting rights strategies identified are illustrated here with the corresponding stories in the countries mentioned, including the United Kingdom, the United States, and some other ex-British colonies in the

TABLE 2.3. *Size of the electorate: The 'Nordic' model*

Country	Voting rights requirements	Electors as % of total population	Percentage points increase
Germany			
1871–1917	Adult (age 25) men	18–22	
1918–1933	Adult (age 20) men and women	64–68	+44
....			
1946–1971	Adult men and women	67	
1972	Men and women (age 18)	70	+3
Sweden			
1866–1909	Adult (age 25) men, with property or income	6–7	
1910–1920	Adult (age 24) men	20	+13
1921–1940	Adult (age 23) men and women	55–65	+35
1941–1969	Adult (age 21) men and women	68–69	+3
1970–1973	Men and women (age 19)	70	+1
1974–	Men and women (age 18)	72–76	+4
Norway			
1814–1896	Adult (age 25) male family chiefs	5–9	
1897–1906	Adult (age 24) men	20	+11
1907–1912	Adult men and some women	32–34	+12
1913–1918	Adult men and women	46	+12
1919–1945	Adult (age 23) men and women	51–62	+5
1946–1968	Adult (age 21) men and women	68	+6
1969–1977	Adult (age 20) men and women	69	+1
1978–	Men and women (age 18)	73–76	+4
Finland			
1900–1906	Adult (age 25) men, with property or income	9	
1907–1940	Adult (age 24) men and women	48–50	+49
1944–1969	Adult (age 21) men and women	62	+12
1970–1971	Adult (age 20) men and women	67	+5
1972–	Men and women (age 18)	82	+15

Note and *Sources*: As for Table 2.1. Dotted line indicates as authoritarian period.

'Anglo' model; France, Italy, and Spain in the 'Latin' model; and Germany and the Scandinavian countries in the 'Nordic' model.

The 'Anglo' model

The typical Anglo-American strategy for allocating voting rights is a continuing combination of carrot and stick measures. On the one hand, there is a process of successive moderate enlargements of the electorate by gradually relaxing legal requirements for voting. On the other hand, the rulers introduce new legal or political barriers to the enforcement of voting rights, all of this under the framework of highly restrictive electoral and party systems. The process seeks to prevent the sudden formation of a new alternative majority to the incumbent electorate by permitting only

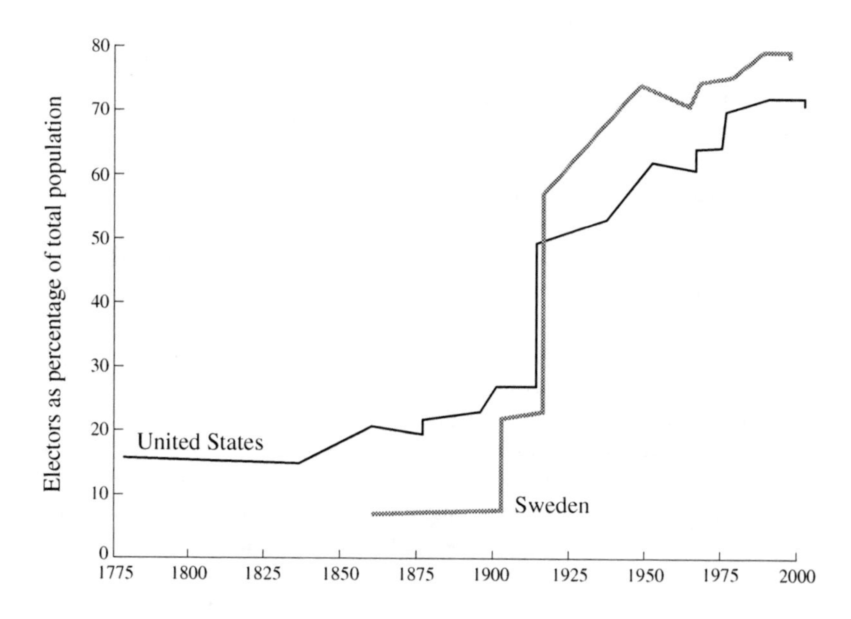

FIG. 2.1. Two strategies of voting rights

a gradual increase in its complexity and by reducing the number of potentially winning alternatives to two.

United Kingdom

The introduction of equal universal suffrage rights in the contemporary United Kingdom took more than one hundred years. Until the early 19th century, as has been sketched in the previous section, British elections were based upon the enfranchisement of a relatively low number of local communities (counties and boroughs) governed by local customs and special provisions which created virtual universal male suffrage in a number of places. A series of Electoral Reform Acts enacted in 1832, 1867, and 1885 established increasingly homogen-eous rules across the British territories, gradually resulting in an enlarged franchise, but also introducing some new restrictions on electoral representation. Later, women's suffrage was approved in a two-stage process: 1918 and 1928. Certain remnants of old distortions, like the plural vote, were not abolished until 1948 (Seymour 1915; Seymour and Frary 1918; Conacher 1971; Cox 1987).

We can examine the permissive and restrictive elements of this series of reforms separately. The two basic elements introduced to create a more complex electorate were the following: higher numbers of voters, a more proportional distribution of seats across the territory, and the reduction of corrupt practices.

First, the number of voters was gradually increased in the first three stages mentioned (1832, 1867, and 1885) by successively co-opting new groups of voters. These new groups amounted to only about 1 per cent, 4 per cent, and 6 per cent of the total population, respectively (see Table 2.1). Specifically, in 1832 new legal requirements in counties and boroughs delimited the electorate to men inhabiting houses worth more than some minimum value, as well as to certain categories of copyholders [*sic*], leaseholders, and tenants. Yet, 'if the borough electorate in the years surrounding the 1832 Reform Act was open and popular it became less so in subsequent years [1841–66] as demographic change led to a relative diminution of adult male voters' (Taylor 1997: 70).

To counteract this evolution, a high number of householders in the boroughs were enfranchised in 1867. However, the representatives of the rural boroughs could still outvote the members of industrial districts in the Midlands, the Northwest, and the North. A uniform regulation of household requirements was finally established in 1885, with particularly inclusive results in certain urban counties. Parallel to these new enfranchisements, a number of nonresident borough voters, however previously qualified, were disfranchised.

Second, new distributions of parliamentary seats to the disadvantage of the boroughs and Southern counties and in favor of urban and industrial areas gradually approached a closer correspondence of political representation to the distribution of population. As a result of these reforms, at the end of the 19th century the British electorate amounted to about 15 per cent of the total population. Some demographic changes expanded its numbers to almost 20 per cent during World War I. In 1918, there was a first partial enfranchisement of women who were either 30 years of age, owners of land, or wives of voters, introducing a new quarter of the total population into the electorate. As previously discussed, it was expected that most of the new female voters would vote similarly to 'their fathers and husbands' in the middle and upper classes of the society. Literally, certain Conservative leaders expected the enfranchisement of women to be a counterweight to the votes of working-class men. Universal adult women's suffrage was completed ten years later and an additional portion of about 15 per cent of the total population was added.

Third, the introduction of the secret ballot in 1872, as well as new regulations regarding campaign expenses and corrupt practices in 1883, allowed new voters to express their political preferences more sincerely than before. With the previous practice of viva voce voting, the decision of each elector was often recorded together with his name, thus allowing the opportunity for bribery or intimidation and checking the votes. It was during only the late 1880s that these practices were seriously curbed.

The restrictive elements introduced by successive reforms can be summarized as follows. First, for the first time a system of voters' registration was created in 1832. The requirements for a person to be put on the electoral lists were so complicated that a very large proportion of individuals who were actually qualified did not become voters. Many people were victims of residential or rate-paying requirements, other people's objections, or the numerous bureaucratic complexities involved. The power of official electoral agents identified with the interests of incumbent voters in making the electoral lists did not give way to party activists' pressures and decisions by an impartial tribunal until the very end of the century.

Second, plural vote was gradually replaced with equal vote for every individual. Yet, more than one-tenth of the electorate still held more than one vote on the basis of their property or education qualifications after the 1885 reforms. Between forty and eighty seats in each election were determined by those voters. Some business people and members of university communities held dual votes until 1948.

Third, the electoral system remaind based upon plurality rule, which allows overrepresentation to the largest parties and reduces or eliminates the role of any other parties. In addition, there were some significant restrictive reforms. Until 1885, most districts elected two representatives, which, on the basis of loose parties and the correspondingly relevant role of candidates' personal standing, permitted a somewhat varied representation of the electorate. In 1867, the introduction of the limited vote in a few three- and four-member districts promoted multiparty-coalition candidacies, while a number of voters tended to split their votes among candidates of different parties, thus creating some pluralistic representation. However, these practices were curbed in 1885 by the establishment of single-member districts inducing, single-party vote.

Fourth, local candidates and political elites were gradually replaced with national party leadership. A crucial institutional development was the centralization of legislative power in the Cabinet, which induced more cohesive party voting in the House of Commons. As individual members of parliament became less powerful and nationwide party organization and discipline increased, national leaders were able to nominate party candidates in elections, and voters usually adapted to the narrow choice offered by a two-party system. In fact, more cohesive parties in a two-party system diminished the scope of possible choices of candidates by the electorate.

Conservatives and Liberals dominated British political life during the 19th century, while minority Radicals promoted more pluralistic forms of representation unsuccessfully. Eventually, a new potential majority gradually emerged, not as a sudden replacement of any of the two existing dominant parties, but through intermediate stages involving, first, electoral coalitions between the Liberals and labor representatives and, later, the split of the Liberal party (by Lloyd George's faction). When, on the grounds of a larger electorate, the Labour party obtained some success at the polls in the 1920s and Labour leaders forecast a possible party victory under the existing electoral rules, they turned against its former proposals for proportional representation. The existing rules thus allowed a significant change in the two major parties by replacing the Liberals with the

Labourites, and, finally, the institutional system was capable of reinforcing its most restrictive features.

United States

The process of allocating voting rights has been even slower and more restrictive in the United States than in the United Kingdom. Initially, as mentioned in the previous section, some British regulations of voting rights during the colonial era, especially those requiring land ownership, produced a much greater enfranchisement in the British colonies in North America than in Britain because of the colonies' widespread diffusion of land-property. Yet, starting with an electorate as large as more than 15 per cent of the total population prior to independence, a very slow process of gradual enlargements of the electorate developed during the subsequent two hundred years.

The basic stages of the enlargement of the electorate included: the suppression of property or tax requirements for adult men to vote during the 19th century, the enfranchisement of women in 1920, the enfranchisement of African–Americans, first in the North after the Civil War in the 1870s and later in the South in the 1960s, as well as the inclusion of young voters in the 1970s. This series of successive limited enlargements was accompanied by parallel measures aimed at demobilizing voters and reducing the scope of their political choice, especially regarding immigrants at the turn of the 19th and 20th centuries, and at reinforcing the two-party system.

Between independence and the Civil War, a variety of state regulations were passed that can be summarized as follows: fourteen states holding land ownership requirements for voting eventually replaced them with less stringent qualifications. The process of abolishing land requirements started in 1778 (in South Carolina) as was completed in 1856 (in North Carolina). Typically, real estate property requirements gave way to personal property alternatives, taxpaying, and then to no limitations. However, at least five states required tax qualifications for voting until 1870. Residence requirements varied from six months to one or two years, although aliens were permitted to vote in six states. Universal women's vote was suppressed in New Jersey in 1807 while a limited number of voting women with property (including widows in particular) were banned from the polls in Massachusetts, New York, and other states, and from voting in local elections in most of the ex-provinces—all of this against the usual practices of the colonial period. In eight of the former colonies and in eleven Southern states of the Union, as well as in the newly created states, African–Americans were excluded from voting (they could vote in only six states in New England). Also, soldiers, students, the mentally ill, the poor, and criminals were denied access to suffrage in most states.

This process, made up of both permissions and restrictions, was led not only by pressures from the excluded, and cautious calculations by the incumbent voters and leaders, but also by competition among states. One state would abandon, for example, the property test, in order to retain workers that were attracted by new enfranchising rules in another state; certain states in the Midwest tried to attract immigrants from other states by agreeing to let them vote; and a border state between the South and the North would oppose African–Americans' suffrage because of fear that many of them would flee from the highly restrictive laws in their native Southern states (Porter 1969).

African–Americans were legally enfranchised in most states only after the Civil War. However, they remained actually disfranchised in the eleven Southern states. In addition, eighteen states introduced literacy tests between 1890 and 1926, with restrictive effects directed in three cases against African–Americans, in five against Indians, Mexicans, and Asians, and in six against recent European immigrants (especially Irish and Germans) (Riker1965: 59–60). In a similar vein, seven states increased the length of their residence requirements. These measures were particularly restrictive in a period when about one-fourth of the male adult population was foreign born and about 10 per cent was nonwhite.

A countermeasure that was perhaps even more effective was found with the generalization of voluntary registration of voters. Only three states had adopted this device by the early 1800s. But most Northern states introduced voluntary registration between 1876 and 1912, up to thirty-one states had followed by 1920, and almost all of them instituted it in the following decade. Typically, the states required annual, in-person registration to allow citizens to enter the electoral lists. This barrier was particularly powerful at the turn of the century in preventing uneducated immigrants in the North and blacks in the South from becoming regular voters and has maintained significant effects regarding immigrants in more recent times (Piven and Cloward 1988).

The set of restrictive measures directed against immigrants, blacks, and other people paying relatively high costs for voluntary registration, implemented at the end of the 19th century, are usually referred to as 'the great disfranchisement'. They seem to have been crucial in preventing the formation of a socialist party strongly based with industrial workers, in marked contrast to Britain and most advanced countries of the time.

Women were gradually given (or restored) voting rights in a number of states, beginning with Colorado in 1893, and ending in 1920 with national recognition of their rights. As discussed earlier, some of the suffragists' arguments pointed out the potentially countervailing role of new female voters regarding more unpredictable or threatening groups of disfranchised men. In the North it was expected that women's suffrage might help maintain the political supremacy of incumbent voters because there were more native-born women, likely to replicate their male counterparts' electoral behavior, than recent immigrants, men and women combined. In fact, by introducing formal citizenship requirements, no state permitted aliens to vote since 1928. In the South, similar effects of women's suffrage were expected due to the fact that there were more white women than blacks of both sexes (Kraditor 1968: 18–19, 261–5).

Poll taxes and literacy tests were prohibited in national elections only in 1964, allowing most African–Americans in the eleven Southern states to have access to the polls for the first time. Residence requirements were lowered to 30 days in 1970. And, in parallel to similar decisions in most democracies, 18-year-olds were co-opted to the electorate a year later.

As a consequence of this lengthy process of carrot and stick measures, about 20–25 per cent of the United States' total population was enfranchised between 1870 and 1920, while most immigrants and blacks remained excluded. With the countervailing enfranchisement of women, enfanchisment rose to between 50 and 55 per cent from 1920, and it reached between 60 and 70 per cent only after 1964. Registration procedures, however, have moved only between two-thirds and three-fourths of legally qualified citizens to become registered voters, with the result that only about a half of the total population is actually enlisted in the polls.

Electoral participation has also been discouraged by the institutional restrictions of the electoral system and the limited choice offered by a stable, rigid two-party system. Before the Civil War, third parties obtained an average of 15 per cent of the vote in national elections for the House of Representatives. Even after the emergence of the Republican party as the other major party together with the Democrats in the mid 19th century, third parties maintained regular organizations, won state legislatures, elected governors, and sent delegates to the Presidential electoral college. During the 19th century and into the early 20th century, minor parties had a significant influence on the political agenda by introducing issues, such as the abolition of slavery, income tax, immigration laws, protection of agriculture, prohibition of alcoholic beverages, regulation of working hours, etc.

Yet, in addition to the constraints created by an electoral system in which 'the winner takes all' and by the typical bipolarization produced by presidential elections, further measures against third parties were introduced from 1892. These included restrictions to ballot access, denial of pre-election financial subsidy, denial of media access, and persecution of radical leaders. Local and state party machines pre-empted representative offices against intruders. The national average vote for third parties in House elections went down to 4 per cent in the first half of the 20th century and less than 1 per cent in the second half. Nevertheless, an array of less durable third candidacies, such as those of the Progressives, the State-Rights Democrats, and a number of independent candidates for President, have revealed some broad dissatisfaction with the political supply provided by the two dominant parties (Rosenstone, Behr, and Lazarus 1996; author's own calculations with data in Gillespie 1992).

Voter turnout gradually declined in the first decades of the 20th century (down to 8 per cent of the electorate in the mid term election of Congress in 1942). It increased in the first fifteen years after the World War II, but has suffered a steady decline since 1960 until reaching about 50 per cent in Presidential elections and 30 per cent in mid term Congress elections by the end of the 20th century.

of social security on the grounds that 'the exclusion of the working mass . . . has always the effect of exposing them to the suggestions of revolutionary parties and subversive ideas', whereas political participation, in contrast, develops in them an interest in the maintenance of the state. Giolitti's government designed a reform to multiply the electorate by two, while relying upon a relatively high degree of abstention among new voters. On this basis, the Liberals expected that the traditional practice of coalition-building through *transformismo* would be extended to new popular representatives and would neutralize innovating pressures. Accordingly, in 1913, voting rights were given to all men over the age of 21 able to read and write, as well as to a small group of men over 30 who had undergone military service (Giolitti 1967, ch. 10).

However, in 1918, immediately after the war, mass electoral enfranchisement was implemented by a new Radical government to include all men over 21 and any ex-soldiers under this age. As a consequence of the two reforms, the electorate jumped from 2.5 million to 11.5 million people, a multiplication of the pre-war number of voters by almost five and an addition of 25 per cent of the total population. Both the supporters and foes of universal suffrage coincided in seeing the creation of an electorate so large and new as a challenge to the stability of the previous political order.

As mentioned earlier, the incumbent rulers were poorly organized; they were also divided among themselves, especially because of their differing positions regarding the war, and they proved unable to adapt to and absorb the new voters. Instead, two incompatible and extreme alternatives developed. On the left, the Socialists were led by maximalist leaders in favor of revolution and the establishment of a dictatorship of the proletariat. Just after the war, the Italian Socialist party joined the Communist International led by the Russian Bolsheviks, condemned collaboration with the 'bourgeois state' in any form, and demanded 'all power' for the workers. On the right, and at about the same time, the Pope cancelled the more than forty-year-long prohibition on Catholics participating in Italian political affairs as either voters or candidates, while retaining his rejection of the Italian state. The new Popular party began to mobilize Catholics and large groups of peasants against the establishment.

The results of the first election with universal men's suffrage in 1919 were astonishing in the eyes of most participants and observers. The two new, extreme parties, the revolutionary Socialists and the anti-Italian state Catholics, together gathered more than half popular votes and parliamentary seats. For the Socialists, electoral success was only viewed as a means of expediting the destruction of Parliament and 'the organs of bourgeois domination'. They supported industrial strikes and factory occupation in the North of Italy and engaged in parliamentary sabotage. The Catholics, meanwhile, organized land seizures in the Center and the South and, not being a cohesive party, they were unable to commit themselves to any governmental collaboration (Seton-Watson 1967; Farnetti 1978; Noiret 1994; Clark 1996).

The next election in 1921 produced about the same results with the significant novelty of a group of Fascist deputies being elected. No stable majority government could be formed with such hazardous electoral results produced by a sudden mass enfranchisement. Social conflict, violence, and political bipolarization rapidly increased. A Fascist dictatorship was established for more than twenty years, which eventually led to an open civil war. (For the common characterization of the political conflict in the mid 1940s as a civil war by historians from both the right and the left, see, respectively, Pisano 1965–6 and Pavone 1991.)

Spain

Four major attempts to introduce suddenly universal suffrage in Spain during modern times failed. The first attempt in favor of large-scale men's suffrage was made during the war against Napoleon for elections held between 1810 and 1813. The so-called Constitution of Cádiz, approved in 1812, formally established virtual universal men's suffrage for those aged over 25 and became 'the classical liberal constitution in Latin Europe in the early 19th century' (Carr 1966: 94). About 28 per cent of the total population was enfranchised, the largest proportion of a country's population ever having been given voting rights in the modern world at that time. The same rules were re-established in 1820 and in 1836, but they were suppressed by military *pronunciamentos* induced by authoritarian monarchs.

The second attempt took place in 1869 at the initiative of the Liberals and Republicans previously excluded from legal political activity. A new constitutional monarchy based upon parliamentary elections by universal male suffrage was very soon followed by an even shorter-lived Republic, which was abolished by another *coup d'état*. Liberal political parties were at that time very weak. Traditionalist Catholic monarchists (*Carlists*) on the right and radical anti-clerical republicans (*exaltados*) on the left, promoting incompatible regime alternatives, were able to produce permanent political instability.

A much more durable political regime was established with the restoration of the monarchy by the Conservatives in 1874. Initially, the electorate was limited to about 5 per cent of the total population. The central government was able to control elections by promoting official candidates and organizing fraud through the administration of justice and the prefects. In parallel, a number of local bosses (*caciques*) developed relations of patronage with voters by distributing private benefits (including public employment) in exchange for political support, with the help of bureaucrats, judicial officers, mayors, and provincial governors. These restrictions to political participation and competition induced the development of extra-parliamentary, anti-system political movements, including Anarchism (Romero 1973; Varela 1977; Tusell 1991).

A resumption of the coalition of ostracized Liberals and Republicans for local elections in the mid 1880s appeared as a major challenge and threat to the Conservative rulers, leading them to co-opt the Liberals into the regime by allowing their temporary access to the Cabinet. The Liberals, led by Práxedes-Mateo Sagasta, then tried to incorporate a fraction of the Republicans into their own candidacies by introducing universal men's suffrage, while maintaining a restrictive electoral system mostly based upon single-member districts and plurality rule. In 1890, voting rights were given to all men aged 25 with two-years' residence and other minor restrictions. The new electorate encompassed about one-fourth of the total population, that is, the number of voters was multiplied by five at one shot, almost half of them being illiterate.

Control of elections by the central government weakened, but the role of local networks increased, including new practices of direct purchase of votes. By these means, the incumbent rulers were able to delay the potentially explosive effects of the sudden enfranchisement of a politically uninformed, unorganized electorate under a restrictive electoral and political system. Turnout was only about 50 per cent in the 1890s. However, in 1893, anti-system Republicans won the election in Madrid, in 1901, Republicans and Catalan Regionalists won in Barcelona, and new victories of Republicans in Valencia, as well as Republicans and Socialists in Bilbao, and other cities followed. A new electoral law approved in 1907 by the government of the reformist Conservative Antonio Maura made corrupt practices more difficult and reduced the role of local *caciques*. Turnout rose to 70 per cent in the 1910s, giving Republicans, as well as Regionalists and Socialists, increasing proportions of votes (Ull 1976).

The Liberals, with the support of the Republicans and Socialists, passed a proposal in Parliament for introducing proportional representation in 1919 and again in 1921. On both occasions, the Conservative Government began to prepare the corresponding bill which could have created a more pluralistic, integrative framework (Tusell 1997). But the process failed when the King and military reacted to social unrest with a *coup d'état* and the establishment of a dictatorship in 1923.

The fourth opportunity for universal suffrage was created, in counter-reaction, with the proclamation of the Second Republic in 1931 by a leftist coalition of Republicans and Socialists. Voting rights were extended to women one year later. A majoritarian electoral system promoted increasing political polarization between two blocs supporting incompatible regime alternatives, as will be discussed in the next chapter. In 1936, a new military coup resulted in a civil war which ended with the victory of General Franco's dictatorship. It was only in 1977 that universal suffrage was successfully established in Spain, together with proportional representation in a new parliamentary monarchy (Colomer, 1995*a*).

The 'Nordic' Model

The 'Nordic' strategy of voting rights coincides with the 'Latin' one in that it implements a sudden massive enfranchisement of voters, in contrast to the gradual, step-by-step model in 'Anglo' countries. Yet, unlike the 'Latin' model, the introduction of universal suffrage in Germany, Sweden, and other Northern European countries, typically at the initiative of the political right, has been parallel with the establishment of pluralistic institutional frameworks which permit a multiparty system to exist. This gave way to large multiparty coalitions and relative moderate Cabinets. Democratic stability was thus achieved on the basis of matching a new complex electorate with pluralistic institutional arrangements.

Germany

At the time of the unification of German territories in the second half of the 19th century, the introduction of universal suffrage by the political left under the French model had failed. Following the short-lived liberal period between 1848 and 1850, Prussia (which embraced about two-thirds of German territories and population) was organized as a three-class corporative system. Landowners and financiers chose a third of the representatives, owners of small businesses and public officials chose another third, and workers selected the remaining third. Voting rights were acknowledged within each group to men aged over 24. Representatives were indirectly chosen by electors chosen in single-member districts by majority rule using public ballot. There was universal suffrage for the election of the local Diets in only a few of the small states of the Empire, including in particular Baden and Würtemberg (in the latter case with proportional representation) (Seymour and Frary 1918, vol. 2).

It was the rightist Chancellor Otto von Bismarck who outbid the Liberals by proposing an immediate introduction of universal men's suffrage for the North German Confederation in 1867, and for the Imperial Parliament (*Bundestag*) in 1871. The Chancellor, who at that time was accused of 'opportunism' for embracing his rivals' program, had sophisticated motives for this unexpected proposal. First, Bismarck had been pressured and enticed to introduce universal suffrage during a series of private meetings with the Socialist leader, Ferdinand Lassalle. The two leaders thought that this could curb the Liberal majority in the incumbent Prussian Parliament by promoting, on the one hand, the peasants' and lower-middle class vote for the Conservatives and, on the other, the workers' vote for the Socialists. Also, with this proposal Bismarck eluded a new challenge by Austria to strengthen the German–Austrian Confederation (to the detriment of Prussian domination) under a nondemocratic regime.

The most significant institutional element to contain the political consequences of the new large electorate was the absence of parliamentary control of the Cabinet. The Chancellor (or chief executive) was not chosen by the lower chamber, but by the federal upper chamber (*Bundesrat*), which was not directly elected but appointed by the component states of the German Empire and by its President, the Emperor. Also, this design was based on Bismarck's prudent calculations. As he said in his memoirs, 'The measuring of the limits within such a struggle [of the conservative Government with Parliament and freedom of the press] must be confined, if the control of the government, which is indispensable to the country, is neither to be checked nor allowed to gain a complete power, is a question of political tact and judgement' (for his motives for introducing universal suffrage, see Bismarck 1899: 65–9).

Majority rule with second-round-runoff was again adopted for the election of Parliament, but this time with direct, equal, and secret elections. Under these rules, locally concentrated minorities were able to support different party candidates for the second round in different regions, thus producing a national multiparty system. The Parliament was organized around four basic parties, but about twelve parties regularly obtained representation. Catholics, workers, and farmers developed innovative political mobilization, with an increase in turnout from 50 per cent in 1871 to 85 per cent in 1907–12. Challenged by these new competitors, the Conservatives and Liberals restructured and changed from parties of notables into active mass parties (Ritter 1990*a*, *b*).

After the German defeat in World War I the so-called Weimar Republic was established in 1918. Voting rights were extended to men and women who were 20 years old, together with the introduction of proportional representation, which had previously been supported by the Socialists. The institutional framework of the Empire was adapted to more democratic formulas. The executive branch was made responsible to the lower chamber, but the elected President of the Republic (replacing the previous Emperor) retained significant powers by the appointment of a Chancellor in a 'semi-presidential' relationship. Bipolarization was partly encouraged by the direct election of the President. However, about ten parties obtained representation in Parliament, in such a way that the so-called Weimar coalition, formed by the Christian, Liberal, and Socialist parties, was able to form a majority supporting the regime for most of the period from 1918 to 1930.

Two extreme, anti-system parties, the Communists and the National-Socialists, obtained increasing support until they blocked the formation of centrist coalitions in 1932. However, in the historical perspective sketched here, the rise of the Nazis to government, followed by the suppression of civil liberties, the implementation of racist and war policies, and the establishment of a totalitarian regime, can hardly be attributed to the sudden enlargement of the electorate. In fact, the introduction of universal men's suffrage at the moment of the creation of the German Empire had been followed by more than sixty years of remarkable political stability.

One of the most provoking and controversial interpretations of the electoral success of the Nazis and the suppression of democracy in Germany in the 1930s focuses on the effects of proportional representation, most prominently in the work of Ferdinand A. Hermens (see especially Hermens 1941, ch. 10). Against this link, several points can be made. First, as mentioned, a multiparty system had already existed in Germany for almost fifty years before the introduction of proportional representation. Even if it is true that some of the previously existing political parties were not strongly ideologically oriented, political pluralism and parliamentary coalitions, which developed after 1918, were not an absolute novelty in German politics.

Second, the crucial point in Hermens' argument is that an alternative electoral system based on plurality rule would have prevented the Nazis from obtaining representation when they enjoyed minority popular support and, in this way, it would have made their further growth baseless. However, it can be argued that plurality rule, although it reduces the number of parties, does not always prevent a new, initially small political party from entering into political competition and obtaining representation, as the paradigmatic case of Britain (with the replacement of the Liberals with the Labourites at the turn of the century) clearly shows. New parties are not 'created' by proportional representation, but by political entrepreneurs on the basis of voters' new political preferences engendered from social, economic, and cultural changes. The formation and rise of the National-Socialist party should thus be explained by factors such as certain German ideological traditions, and the party leadership maximalist initiative and organizational effectiveness against the backdrop of Germany's defeat in World War I and its further social disarticulation during the 1920s. Under these inducements, it is highly likely that plurality rule would have worked against centrist parties and increased political bipolarization between the Socialists and Communists on one side and the Nationalists and Nazis on the other, as similar 'majoritarian' electoral systems did in France and Spain, with their own rise of new, extreme parties at about the same time in 1935–6.

In fact, the Nationalists and far right political positions obtained not only a widespread appeal among German voters in the 1920s and early 1930s, but also local strongholds of support in Bavaria as well as in many other regions. It seems reasonable to consider that plurality rule would have made them local winners. Even under proportional representation, the Nazis obtained votes by attracting those who previously supported the Nationalists and other small parties on the right, especially in small cities, partly because they appeared as potential absolute winners at the national level. Plurality rule, which promotes more strategic vote for likely winners than proportional representation, would have reinforced the tendency towards a concentration of votes. If it had any effect, proportional representation might have delayed bipolarization in German politics perhaps for a few months or years. (For a discussion, see Lepsius 1978; Kolb 1988; Nicholls 1991; Feuchtwanger 1993.)

Finally, proportional representation was again adopted with the re-establishment of democracy in West Germany in 1946, despite—or in the memory of—the Weimar experience. The corresponding multiparty system originated a long-lasting practice of coalition governments around the center that consolidated democracy. After the 1966 elections, the Christian-Democrats in government offered the Social-Democrats a change of the electoral system into plurality rule. An independent commission was appointed to this purpose including most remarkably, F. A. Hermens himself, who had returned from the United States a few years earlier. However, the Social-Democrat leadership found the gamble for a two-party system too risky and rejected the proposal, which was also opposed by the smaller Liberal party. (Jesse, 1990). This was a somewhat fortunate decision since the maintenance of a highly proportional representation system was instrumental in making the reunification with the Eastern part of Germany in 1990 feasible by consensual means. It permitted a new enlargement of the elect-orate with differentiated social groups and political preferences, including in particular the ex-Communists as a regular minority party, without major constitutional changes. Political equilibrium remained around moderate Cabinets with center-like policy positions, while the inclusiveness of the system promoted continuous support for democratic stability.

Northern Europe

Sweden, Norway, and Finland experienced processes of sudden introduction of universal suffrage, including, very early on, women's voting rights, together with the enforcement of proportional representation leading to multiparty coalition politics.

In the early 20th century, the Swedish incumbent rulers explicitly exchanged the enlargement of the electorate for a proportional representation electoral system. Previously, Sweden had adopted in 1866 a two-chamber parliament formula supported by very restrictive suffrage rights as an alternative to the traditional four-Estate corporative representation. The new upper chamber was organized on the basis of territorial representation through provincial councils elected by plural vote based on wealth. For the lower chamber, the vote was given to 21-year-old men fulfilling property or income qualifications. Representatives were elected in single-member districts by majority rule. Only between 5 and 8 per cent of the total population was enfranchised in Sweden during the last third of the 19th century. Landowners and farmers dominated political decisions. While the Liberals and the Socialists demanded universal suffrage, the Conservative rulers feared that broadening the franchise would disturb social stability.

However, in the first years of the 20th century, Liberals and Socialists achieved increasing parliamentary representation with the support of the lower-middle class and industrial workers who, because of economic growth, were increasingly able to fulfill the economic requirements for voting. Under plurality or majority rule, this evolution could have produced a total overturn, eventually making the opposition parties absolute winners and the Conservative rulers absolute losers. However, suddenly, and to other actors' and observers' general surprise, the Conservative government led by Arvid Lindman proposed the introduction of universal men's suffrage together with proportional representation in both chambers.

From the incumbent rulers' perspective, a new electoral system permitting multipartism was conceived to be a protective device. The Conservatives would become a minority, but they would not be expelled from the system as might be risked with a majoritarian rule. The incumbent rulers took the initiative of introducing universal suffrage 'with guarantees' rather than witnessing their own defeat. Proportional representation was adopted as an institutional safeguard in place of the traditional safeguards of wealth, property, or income qualifications.

As Lindman reasoned in 1907: 'With universal suffrage and elections in one-man constituencies, the time will not be distant when the interests of farmers here and there in the country are not well represented in elected bodies'. In contrast, with proportional representation, 'the danger of a shift in the direction now indicated is very greatly diminished. Even if farmers are no longer in a majority, agriculture should nevertheless have a chance to enjoy its fair share of representation' (Lewin 1988, ch. 3).

This proposal caused a dramatic reversal of institutional preferences among political parties. Some dissident Liberals joined the Cabinet's proposal, but the Liberal and the Socialist parties' leadership voted against the bill introducing universal suffrage because they refused proportional representation on the basis of their recent optimistic expectations under majority rule. Voting rights for all men over 24 years of age were finally approved in 1909. A few years later, in 1918, a new bill enlarging the electorate to all men and women aged 23 years was also introduced. As a result of these, the Swedish electorate was enlarged in about 50 per cent of the total population, multiplying the number of voters by eight in less than ten years.

The combination of universal suffrage and proportional representation created a very long-lived democratic stability while at the same time confirming to some extent the moderate expectations of the Conservatives. Under the new electoral rules, no single party obtained an absolute majority of seats in Parliament. Until 1930, governments were alternatively led by the Liberals, Socialists, and Conservatives (who returned to power in 1923–4 and again in 1928–30). The emergence of a centrist Agrarian party in the 1920s created a moderating bridge between the two blocs. The Agrarians (nowadays called the Center party) formed coalition Cabinets with the Socialists in the 1930s and the 1950s and with the Liberals and the Conservatives in the 1970s and the 1990s.

A similar, albeit somewhat slower process developed in Norway. A traditional four-Estate corporative representation had been based upon a narrow electorate still encompassing less than 9 per cent of the total population by the 1880s. Indirect elections in multimember districts gave the Norwegian Liberals absolute control of the chamber. Yet the formation of the Labour party in 1887 induced the Liberals to compete more strenuously for popular support. Using the same risk-adverse strategy used by the incumbent Conservative rulers in Sweden, the Norwegian Liberals introduced men's universal suffrage 'from above' in 1897. Women were partly enfranchised in 1907 and given equal electoral rights in 1913.

After the dissolution of the union between Norway and Sweden in 1905, the Norwegian parliament began to be directly elected in single-member districts, with majority rule in the first round and plurality rule in the second round with all previous candidates running again. This formula, while not producing proportional representation, permitted a multiparty system and gave the Liberals the opportunity to remain in power, together with the Conservatives and new Moderates, and to resist the threatening growth of the Labourites. As the electoral decline of the Liberals remained steady, however, they finally introduced proportional representation in 1919.

The results of these institutional reforms positively matched their promoters' basic expectations. No party obtained an absolute majority of seats (leaving room for minority Cabinets relying upon other parties for support). Liberals, Conservatives, and Agrarians alternated as the head of Cabinets against the largest Labour party until the first of a series of Labour governments was formed in 1935. A new reform for a more proportional representation formula (modified Sainte Laguë instead of d'Hondt) in the 1950s resumed the previous alternation of parties allowing once more the non-Socialist parties to share power.

The case of Finland corresponds even better to certain features of the 'Nordic' model previously identified. Since 1863, the Finnish corporative four-Estates had begun to be convened regularly under the control of the Russian Empire. They were elected with a highly restricted franchise, however, elections in multimember districts permitted some political pluralism. The Swedes, who were concentrated in Southern and Western Finland, predominated in the Estate of the nobility and also in the Estate of the burgesses for most of the 19th century. Yet by the end of the century, the Finns predominated in the Estate of burgesses as well as in those of the clergy and farmers, giving them control over parliamentary legislation (since the decision of three out of the four Estates was required). Almost all political groups promoted a modern unicameral parliament in order to fend off Russian domination. When the Swedes' leaders realized that this new institutional framework was going to be adopted, they held out for a system of proportional representation as the only guarantee of the continued representation of minorities in parliament. Since no party then had expectations of achieving an absolute majority of seats by plurality or majority rule, the proposal was accepted.

In 1905, virtually overnight, a unicameral parliament based on universal suffrage of men and—for first time in Europe—also women, was established in Finland, together with an electoral system of proportional representation. About 40 per cent of the total population was introduced into the electorate at one shot, multiplying the existing electorate by more than five. With this highly innovative, pluralistic framework, the Finns were able to confront the continued interference of the Russian Tsarist regime in their local politics, survive the Russian Bolshevik revolution and the following civil war, and achieve independence and a new Constitution in 1919. Since then, multiparty coalition Cabinets have been formed, mostly led by either the Agrarians or Social-Democrats (or both), with the minority Liberals and Swedes (the Swedish People's party) being very frequent partners with both the right and the left (Carstairs 1980, chs 9–11).

3

How Votes Are Counted

> The race is over!
> But who has won?
> Everybody has won, and all must have prizes.
> Lewis Carroll, *Alice's Adventures in Wonderland* (1865)

In relatively simple, homogeneous communities, simple voting and decision rules producing a single, absolute winner are usually chosen. Single-winner rules, such as unanimity, qualified-majority, simple majority, or plurality, dominated the history of voting and elections until the 19th century. They have survived in countries with several-centuries-old political institutions and are still a common institutional choice in small, relatively undifferentiated communities.

In pre-modern times many supporters of these rules considered them as devices for discovering the truth, be it called God's will or the People's will. They expected that the social choice obtained with those rules would be widely accepted and very stable. This expectation is quite reasonable in the context of simple communities whose members may not have very disparate preferences on a small number of issues. They can be aggregated into a single enforceable decision without much effort. However, in large, complex societies in which a high number of policy issues arise and are submitted to binding collective decisions, single-winner rules tend to produce a highly uneven distribution of political satisfaction between winners and losers, and low social utility. As a consequence of the incentives created for the absolute losers to try to overthrow such unfavorable decisions, single-winner rules may also induce instability of the social choice.

Modern utilitarian reasoning aimed at achieving the greatest satisfaction of the greatest number of people inspired the search for alternative voting rules. They include those producing multiple winners, such as proportional representation and other institutional devices favoring negotiations and agreements between differentiated groups. Multiple-winner rules distribute satisfaction more widely among the different groups of a society, and tend to produce more consensual and stable decisions and higher social utility than single-winner rules.

Social choice theory can help to make the basic intuition sketched in the previous paragraphs more precise. The questions identified here will also guide formal and empirical analyses of the working of different voting rules in real-world politics.

According to social choice models, for a given electorate the stability and efficiency of the social choice heavily depends on: (i) the number of issue-dimensions which are prominent at voting; and (ii) the number of available alternatives to be voted for (in the form of candidates, parties, policy proposals, bill amendments, etc.).

When voters' preferences can be formed along a single issue-dimension, such as the typical left–right ideological axis, the social optimum coincides with the median voter's preference. The median, that is, the point with no more than a half of voters on both its right and its left, minimizes the sum of distances from the voters' preferences and, therefore, can be considered to maximize social utility.

Efficient outcomes can be achieved by single-winner rules, such as majority or plurality rules, if only two alternatives are available, since the winner can be expected to have the support of the median voter. However, likely losers in a relatively simple issue space can have incentives to introduce new issues and new alternatives in order to alter the outcome in their favor. By the creation of a multidimensional space of issues, new winners and instability of the social choice will appear. The outcome can become unpredictable and move away from the socially efficient median point. The more inclusive the rule (the most inclusive one being unanimity), the more new issues and alternatives are needed to destabilize the winner. The more exclusive the rule, such as simple plurality, the more potentially unstable, arbitrary, and inefficient the winner can be as a consequence of former losers' new strategies. In contrast, multiple-winner rules, such as proportional representation and the subsequent negotiation process, tend to organize multiparty coalitions around the alternative supported by the median voter.

In this chapter we will explore whether and how different voting rules create incentives for actors' strategies to develop new issues, new alternatives, confrontation, or negotiation which can lead to more or less efficient and stable social choices.

In particular, two characteristics of voting rules that have been targeted by social choice theory will be discussed. The so-called 'monotonicity' condition requires that a voting rule does not put at a disadvantage an alternative obtaining more support among the voters. We will examine whether votes and seats maintain 'monotonic' relations under different voting rules, that is, whether both increase or decrease in parallel. Specifically, situations in which one alternative becomes the winner despite having obtained less popular support in votes than some other alternative will be considered clear and blatant cases of nonmonotonicity.

The second condition is known in social choice theory as 'independence of irrelevant alternatives'. Basically, it states that the winning alternative should not depend on how many other alternatives are available at some particular moment of decision making. If one nonwinning alternative ceases to be available, the outcome should be unchanged as long as individual preferences over the remaining alternatives do not change. The lack of fulfillment of this condition for a voting rule makes it vulnerable to such well-known strategies as 'divide and win' and 'merge and win'. In general, minority winners and, more precisely, minority winners located at an extreme position on the issue space, will be considered as lacking this desirable property since they could be beaten by a potential majority if the appropriate alternative existed.

The Efficient Median Voter

The frequency of winners supported by the median voter with different voting rules is analyzed for 451 parliamentary and presidential elections in forty countries for the period 1945–2000 in Table 3.1. We consider 'winners' the party or parties in the Cabinet in parliamentary regimes and the party or parties supporting the President in popular elections in presidential and semi-presidential regimes. Roughly speaking, median voter's Cabinets and median voter's Presidents were produced in slightly more than half (54 per cent) of the elections by plurality rule and almost three-fourths (73 per cent) of the elections by majority rule (or qualified-plurality rule in a few presidentialist countries). In contrast, Cabinets based on proportional representation have the support of the median voter in more than 90 per cent of the cases. Most of the countries in the list that elect representatives with proportional representation and have parliamentary regimes have *always* included the median voter's party in the Cabinet (in 138 elections in ten countries).

This allows us to state that the outcomes of elections producing multiple winners with proportional representation are relatively more socially efficient than those of elections with single-winner rules. Among the latter, the more inclusive the rule, as is majority compared to plurality rule, the more efficient the social choice.

Voters' preferences can be identified on the basis of their voting or by using opinion surveys. Some simplification of issue preferences is needed to make comparisons feasible. In fact, voters and leaders themselves usually proceed to this kind of simplification in order to communicate political messages along a single dimension, such as the typical left–right scale, which usually synthesizes voters' varied preferences, political party platforms, and governmental agendas on many issues. The available evidence shows that most citizens in most democratic countries can place

outcome. But this is likely to be socially inefficient, as well as highly unstable since it can be replaced with some other alternative with relatively small innovations.

The trade-off thus works as follows. The more inclusive the rule (such as unanimity), the more consensual and efficient, but the less effective in producing outcomes it will be. The more exclusive the rule (such as simple plurality), the more effective it will be, but more inefficient outcomes will be produced. The above-mentioned voting rules, as well as other intermediate rules, such as qualified-majorities or qualified-pluralities that are also found in a number of real-world political institutions, will be analyzed for their results regarding these important aspects of social choice.

Unanimity

Unanimity rule is usually considered to be a procedure favoring consensual decisions. By definition, a unanimous decision requires the agreement of all and must be considered to be better for all voters than the status quo or the absence of a decision. In this sense, unanimity outcomes are considered to be 'Pareto superior' than any alternative occurrence and they certainly fulfill the monotonicity condition.

However, if voters' preferences can be located along a single dimension, unanimity rule leads to immobility. No decision can be made to alter the status quo because any voter can veto a move away from his preference. Initially advantaged voters (those whose preferences are closer to the status quo) can consolidate their privileges. The outcome will remain stable independently of its distance from the social optimum located on the median of voters' preferences.

With the introduction of new issues or new values of judgement creating a multidimensional space, several unanimous decisions can be made available from the initial status quo. But each one of the possible decisions will give different voters different degrees of satisfaction of their preferences and will produce different amounts of social utility. Since costly negotiations can be needed to achieve a single decision, the cost of making decisions or the control of the agenda may produce biased and socially inefficient outcomes.

Bias and Inefficiency

The biases in social efficiency of the outcomes produced by unanimity rule in a multidimensional space can be illustrated with the help of Fig. 3.1. From the initial status quo point (SQ), unanimity decisions by voters A, B, and C are possible in favor of any alternative located inside the lens-shaped area in the figure. This area is formed by circular indifference curves

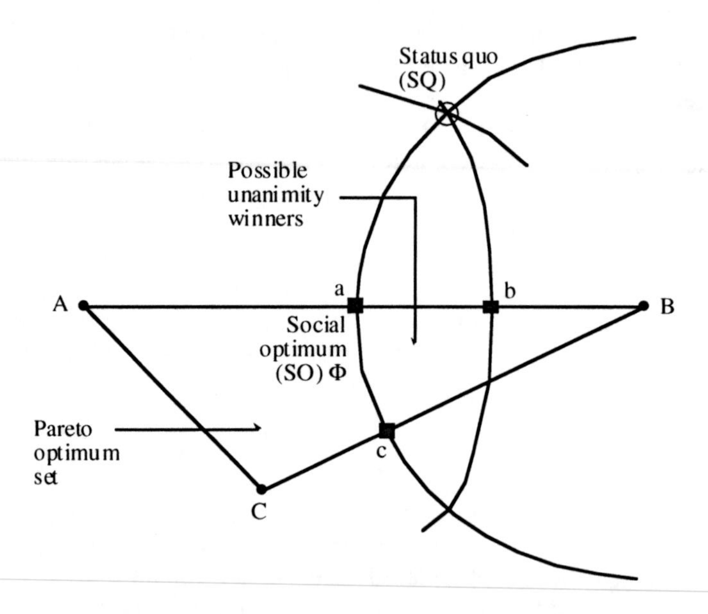

FIG. 3.1. Decisions with unanimity rule

around the voters' preferences A, B, and C that pass through the initial point SQ. All the points in this area are preferred by all voters because they are a shorter distance from the voters' preferences than SQ.

The set of possible decisions by unanimity intersects with the Pareto optimum set, which is the minimal set containing all voters' preferences (the triangle A B C). Any outcome within this intersection (the shaded area) is stable because none of the points in the area can be beaten by unanimity by any other alternative. No new unanimity can be obtained in favor of a move from it because at least one voter would find the new proposal less satisfactory and would veto it.

The set of stable winners by unanimity may or may not include the social optimum point (SO). As can be seen, SO is not included in the set of unanimity winners in Fig. 3.1. Only if the status quo is very distant from the voters' preferences, that is, the initial state is very unsatisfactory for the voters, will the social optimum point be within the set of stable decisions by unanimity. Precisely, the social optimum point can only be reached by a unanimous decision from an initial status quo placed outside an area which is at least three times larger than the Pareto optimum set. If the initial status quo is closer to the voters' preferences or less unsatisfactory (as in Fig. 3.1), only socially nonoptimum decisions can be made. From highly unsatisfactory initial states, dramatic changes leading to highly satisfactory and stable outcomes are feasible; from less unsatisfactory initial states, mediocrity tends to endure (Colomer 1999*a*).

Different voters will prefer different outcomes out of the set of possible unanimity decisions, as shown in Fig. 3.1. Voter A, for example, will prefer the alternative a, while voter B will prefer b, and voter C will prefer c. If voter A is the agenda setter, A can submit the alternative a to voting against the unsatisfactory status quo (SQ). The agenda setter A can expect an agreement on a on the basis of the higher level of satisfaction of all voters' preferences produced by this alternative, the cost for the other voters of negotiating another proposal or replacing the agenda setter, and the pressures of the institutional environment to make an effective, quick decision. In contrast, if voter B is the agenda setter, B will submit the alternative b to voting against the status quo in the expectation of analogous developments in favor of b, etc. A unanimous decision in favor of any of these or the other alternatives located inside the shaded area becomes stable. In this sense, unanimity social choices are dependent on irrelevant alternatives; having different sets of proposals to vote for may produce different winners.

Thus, unanimity rule produces stable social choices. However, the social efficiency of the outcome is highly dependent on the status quo, the distribution of bargaining costs among voters, and the agenda setter's maneuvering. This is significant because on many political issues, including policy choices and other provisions of public goods, the status quo is not typically chosen by voters nor does it necessarily depend on their preferences or on available alternatives. Given the usual existence of several possible outcomes, unanimity social choices are uncertain. The satisfaction they provide is biased in favor of advantaged voters, such as those with the power of making proposals first or those with a greater capacity for paying negotiation costs. Unanimity stable social choices are monotonic and included in the Pareto optimum set, but they may be socially inefficient from the point of view of social utility.

Cases: Medieval Assemblies and International Organizations

Unanimity rule has been enforced in at least two different types of institutions which will be briefly reviewed below. (1) The Christian Church in the Middle Ages and a few medieval parliaments, including in particular the Aragonese and Catalan Corts and the Polish Diet; (2) Most international organizations, with two major examples surveyed here, the United Nations Security Council and the Council of the European Community.

As will be seen, a common pattern can be identified in the evolution of these as well as other political institutions making decisions with unanimity rule. First, some initial socially efficient decisions can be made, in the sense of choosing outcomes that approach the Pareto optimum set of alternatives in which all participants are better off than in the previous status quo. Second, there can be further stagnation and absence of new decisions due to the veto power of every participant, even if the previous outcomes do not correspond to socially optimum solutions. Finally, a change to a nonunanimity rule may be expected in order to regain institutional capability to make efficient social choices.

God's Single Will

Unanimity rule was prevalent in the Christian Church for many centuries, as it was considered to be the only rule that could assure the participants that their decision was right or inspired by God. At the beginning of the Christian era, most bishops were unanimously elected with participation of the Christian faithful ('the people'). The election of a bishop, including the Bishop of Rome whose primacy over the other bishops was only gradually asserted, was conceived as a way to discover God's will. Hence the maxim '*vox populi, vox Dei*', or the 'people's voice is God's voice'.

The Church also restated the Roman law principle (embodied in the Justinian code): 'What concerns similarly all ought to be approved by all', by affirming that 'He who governs all should be elected by all'. Popular participation induced unanimous consent and obedience from the faithful and gave the Church solid ground for expanding its influence and attracting a large following in the first few centuries after Jesus (Benson 1968).

However, dissidence over several candidates for bishop or for pope, as well as the frequent ineffectiveness of unanimity rule in producing a winner, became a source of popular tumult, conflicts, and schisms relatively early. Even before Christianity had been officially accepted by the Roman Emperor, at least one simultaneous election of two different popes had taken place (in 250, after eighteen months of failure to elect). In 366 and 418, the election of two popes by different factions of the Church provoked hundreds of deaths and the intervention of Roman troops. These conflicts put the Church for several centuries under the protection and domination of political powers, especially Italian noble families and emperors. The Church obtained the Emperor's effective renunciation of the right to appoint the pope only at the Concordat of Worms in 1122. The present Catholic Church recognizes 159 Popes from 1 to 1122, but at least thirty-one 'anti-popes' were recognized by certain factions. From the mid 9th to the mid 10th century, twenty-two out of twenty-six popes were overthrown (twelve were removed from office, five sent into exile, and five killed) (author's own calculations with data in Levillain 1994.)

The ineffectiveness of unanimity rule eventually moved the Church to adopt alternative rules. First, the laity was excluded from the election of the pope and voting was reserved for the cardinals (by a Papal Bull in 1059). However, unanimity among the cardinals was also difficult to reach. Priority was then given to the vote of the cardinal-bishops, who were entrusted with gaining the assent of the cardinal-priests and the cardinal-deacons, as well as the approval of the other members of the Church. More ambiguously, the identification of the '*sanior et maior pars*' (the 'sounder and greater part') of voters was introduced in order to persuade some dissidents to support a candidate and create apparent unanimity when it did not exist. Moral qualities like seniority, zeal, and the dignity of voters were considered relevant because voting was conceived as a way to discover the truth. But the 'sanior pars' often did not coincide with the 'maior pars'. In elections of bishops, the determination about which was the 'sanior' part in a divided electorate could be submitted to an arbiter, such as the metropolitan bishop or even the pope, but no such arbiter existed for the election of the pope after the suppression of imperial control. Three 12th-century elections by cardinals under unanimity rule ended in the appointment of two rival candidates which, together with their successors, produced eight anti-popes and only nine 'official' popes in less than fifty years.

Unanimity rule was associated with a mystical and theological notion of the Church's unity. Whereas voters' unanimity was believed to be inspired by God, any failure in obtaining such a total consensus was seen as an instigation of the devil. Nevertheless, the frequency of conflicts led to abandoning unanimity rule and to the adoption of two-thirds majority rule by Pope Alexander III (himself previously in competition with an anti-pope) at the Third Lateran Council in 1179. Alexander III's six-month stay in Venice during 1177, during which he reconciled with the Emperor Frederick Barbarossa who had supported the anti-pope, may well have exposed him to the city's sophisticated voting procedure for electing a doge (sketched in the previous chapter) and induced him to adopt a more effective nonunanimity rule for elections of the Church soon thereafter (Baldwin 1968).

The basic aim of the qualified-majority rule of two-thirds was the formation of a consensual, large coalition of cardinals without giving any of them veto power. The outcome could be considered to be rather stable because, in order to overthrow a winning candidate with two-thirds support, the losers would have to persuade at least *a majority* of the winner's original supporters to change their mind. The expected stability of qualified-majority winners allowed the Church to consider this rule also as a right procedure for discovering God's will. In the words of Pope Pius II about his own election in 1458, 'What is done by two thirds of the sacred college [of cardinals], that is surely of the Holy Ghost, which may not be resisted' (Gragg and Gabel 1959: 88). The rule of two-thirds also came into play in elections of bishops and abbots.

In contrast to the previous history of conflicts and schisms, two-thirds rule was efficacious and did produce rather stable outcomes. However, a qualified-majority rule is still somewhat demanding, which can be effective at the expense of rather long delays in decision making. Under the rule of two-thirds, negotiations to form a sufficiently large coalition to elect the pope caused extremely long vacancies in the Holy See during the 13th century (up to thirty-four months).

This led to establishing the practice of locking up cardinals until they reached a decision, which was formally shaped as the *conclave* (from the Latin: with key), first in 1274 and again from 1294. The cardinals are given incentives to make a quick decision by being submitted to external isolation, certain physical and material restraints, scanty information about candidates, and restricted communication among themselves. This certainly makes qualified-majority rule effective in producing outcomes, but it also leads the cardinals to precipitate decisions driven by the desire to leave such an uncomfortable environment. (For a broader and more detailed discussion, see Colomer and McLean 1998.)

From the 17th to the 19th centuries, the leaders of cardinals' factions in the conclave were based on ecclesiastic orders, political allegiances, or geographical origins. They bartered their support for future appointments or doctrinal reforms. Usually, a committee of independents called the 'flying squad' (*squadra volante*) was formed to bargain with the factions (Lector 1894). Beginning with the 20th century, several prominent issue-dimensions to promote candidates were developed, including progressive-conservative, bishop-Curia member, and Italian-foreigner. The endogenous creation of issues and candidates tends to raise the bargaining costs. This leads cardinals in conclave to look for intuitively appealing focal points, shifting to favor those candidates who obtain increasing support and appear as potential winners in the first rounds of voting. The analysis of voting rounds in modern conclaves shows that any front-runner who loses one vote from one round to the next immediately becomes a 'dead horse'. In contrast, candidates who maintain or increase their votes, even from a very low initial support, can attract particular attention, even if they are not highly consensual or have hardly been mentioned as *papabile* a few hours before being crowned (Colomer 1996*c*).

In sum, the ineffectiveness of the initially adopted unanimity rule was traded off in the Church for the lower consensus of a qualified-majority rule. The latter rule has been relatively more effective. But additional environmental pressures were implemented in order to induce the cardinals to make quick decisions. A number of popes have been elected as a result of these institutional pressures rather than for their proximity to well-informed, sincere preferences of many of the cardinal-voters. Frequent surprises in favor of inefficient candidates gave rise to the popular saying, 'He who enters the conclave a pope, leaves it a cardinal', which has had the status of an 'empirical law' since the 14th century.

Consensual Medieval Parliaments

Medieval kings, emperors, and popes called assemblies of great feudal nobles, ecclesiastical dignitaries, and other notables to ask their counsel or opinion, or simply to highlight new legislative measures, foreign treaties, or dynastic marriages. The Magna Carta conceded by King John of England in 1215 is usually mentioned as the starting point. Representative institutions flourished particularly in the kingdoms and principalities of Latin Europe, including Aragon, Catalonia and Valencia, Leon and Castille, Navarre, Portugal, and Sicily from the 13th century onwards, as well as in France, the German Empire, and the Northern European kingdoms in later periods. While many of these assemblies remained consultative bodies, some of them developed more significant initiatives and decision power and eventually became relevant institutions of government.

The doctrine of unanimous consent emerged from practice. By the late 12th century, not only the Church, as previously discussed, but also some civil powers had adopted virtual unanimity rule by referring to the Roman principle: 'What concerns all ought to be approved by all'. A further evolution, however, moved most of these bodies from 'the primitive unanimity' to alternative criteria, such as the 'sounder and greater part' (already mentioned regarding the Church), qualified-majorities, or simple majority rule (Konopczynski 1930; Marongiu 1968; Wilkinson 1972; Myers 1975).

Two cases corresponding to different periods, the *Cortes* of Aragon from the 13th century and the Polish Diet from the 16th century, are discussed here for their basic similarities: both achieved great control over legislation and both formally adopted unanimity rule for important decisions. Also, in both cases, the requirement of unanimous agreements eroded their capability of decision making and made the parliaments vulnerable to the rule of more effective, less consensual institutions.

The Aragonese and Catalan '*Dissentimiento*'

One of the earliest meetings recorded of a representative assembly in Europe was in 1064, in Barcelona, Catalonia, for the approval by consensus and acclamation of public laws later compiled in the celebrated Customs of the city (*Usatges*). By the middle of the 12th century, the counts of Barcelona also became Kings of Aragon. Beginning in 1162, they summoned regular assembles of representatives of the clergy, the nobles, and the knights, as well as the towns.

The 'General Cortes' developed in parallel to separate meetings of the Cortes of Aragon and the Corts of Catalonia, as well as the Corts of Valencia after its conquest. From the mid-13th century, the Catalan-Aragonese confederation expanded its dominions south into the Iberian Peninsula against the previous Muslim domination, parallel to the expansion of Castille, and became the major power in the Mediterranean. The Aragonese Cortes were the model for the Sicilian and Sardinian parliaments.

The King of Aragon was bound to summon the Cortes once every five years and, after the union with Catalonia, every other year, although the actual calendar of meetings was highly irregular. The business of the Cortes included solving justice disputes (especially 'grievances' or complaints from individuals or towns, concerning the King's officers or other Estates' members), approving legislation, and voting on taxes. For the approval of all the more important laws, the Aragon

Cortes required that each of its four component Estates had to come to a unanimous decision ('*nemine discrepante*'). Every member could veto any decision by his *dissentimiento*. Yet, when total consent was not achieved, the accord was registered as made by '*unanimiter excepto N.N.*', leaving room for further debates and discussions, although they often ended in 'no result'. Eventually, some individual objections were declared to be 'absurd', 'not pertinent', or 'irrational' and the matter was referred to a permanent committee formed by two representatives from each Estate as an arbiter to judge on the soundness of the existing majority will (see the discussion in González Antón 1978).

The Catalan parliament was institutionalized at an assembly in Barcelona in 1283, when a long and formal list of participants was established, including representatives of 'the citizens and men of the towns'. King Peter the Great promulgated a series of legislative decrees to guarantee both the rights of his subjects and just administration, especially in matters of justice and taxation. He committed himself and his descendants to enact any general constitution or statute of Catalonia only with 'the approval and consent' of the prelates, barons, knights, and citizens of the country. The Catalan Corts should have been summoned once a year 'to treat of matters of common utility for the country', but after repetitive delays, triennial convocations were adopted in 1301, although the permanent parliamentary commission, the *Generalitat*, might call Extraordinary Assemblies.

Unanimous agreements were laboriously constructed in the Catalan Corts in several ways, including deliberation; lengthy negotiations within each of the Estates, between solicitors of the different Estates, and between solicitors of the Estates and the King; by attracting voters to the bandwagon in public and ordered voting rounds which started with the higher or 'sanior' parts; and by bribes from the King offering jobs and money to the dissenters.

Yet, given the relative ineffectiveness of unanimity rule in making decisions, the Corts asked the king to interpret the founding constitution as allowing to replace unanimous consent with the opinion of the '*major e de la pus sana part*' in matters of legislation (according to the example of the Castilian Cortes, as well as the Church's practices previously mentioned). Consequently, certain measures were declared valid if they were approved by the nobles' and the citizens' estates with disagreement or abstention of the clerical representatives or by other qualified majorities.

In the Corts of Valencia, unanimity was required for the Estate of nobles. But at least on one occasion, in 1645, unanimity was reached by throwing a recalcitrant member out into the street and then proceeding to a vote.

After the union of the Crowns of Aragon and Castille in the late 15th century, the unanimity-inspired, consensual Cortes were gradually curbed by the Habsburg monarchs of Spain. The Cortes of Aragon abandoned their virtual unanimity rule after 1592, but some of their tasks were transferred to other bodies. The Catalan Corts gathered together in 1626, after twenty-seven years without sessions, but were unable to make a single decision, whether on grievances, legislation, or taxes, thus preparing further constitutional and secessionist conflicts. The Corts held a few more meetings, but were formally suppressed after the victory of the Bourbon dynasty in the Succession War and the corresponding establishment of a 'New Plan', inspired by the French centralized model, in 1716 (Coroleu and Pella 1876; Ferro 1987; Gil 1991).

The Polish '*Liberum Veto*'

The Diet or 'Noble Parliament of Poland' (*Sejm*) worked with unanimity rule from the 16th to the 18th century. The General or Great Diet was formed by the King (elected by the Diet since the late 13th century), the Senate (with up to 150 members), and the Chamber of Deputies (with up to 236 members). Before attending the General Diet the elected deputies gathered together at provincial Diets, where they received compulsory mandates, especially on taxes. According to the procedure formally established by law in 1572, the Diet held ordinary sessions of six weeks every two years. All decisions should be adopted by unanimity ('*nemine contradicente*'), that is, by general agreement of all senators and deputies with every voter enjoying '*liberum veto*'. At each session, all laws were to be approved in a single package. The president of the Chamber, known as the 'marshall', played a prominent role in inducing negotiations and agreements.

During the 16th century, the Polish Diet was able to make unanimous decisions in favor of significant 'modernizing', nationally oriented reforms, such as the expropriation of lords' properties; the creation of new legal institutions, territorial homogenization, and monetary unification; the annexion of Lithuania; affirmation of sovereignty in the face of the German Empire and the Papacy; the declaration of freedom of thought; and the termination of religious wars.

However, from the early 17th century, the ineffectiveness of the Diet began to increase. 'Unended' or 'broken' Diets, that is, biennial sessions where no decision could be made as a result of some member's veto, proliferated. Every deputy or senator could nullify all decisions taken during a session just by using a formula such as 'I declare nullity of the Diet', 'I do not permit', 'I protest', or others. Among the intended remedies to the Diet's decadence, was a suggestion that the debates be prolonged beyond the previously established period of six weeks. But the proposed prolongation had also to be approved by unanimity. From 1669, several vetoes blocked not only proposals to prolong the deliberations but also the ordinary sessions. In 1689, the session ended even before the marshall was appointed. In the words of certain historians, the feeling that 'the sense of public interest was being lost' spread widely. Complaining popular slogans, such as 'Individualism is the master of Poland!', arose. During the 17th century and due to the Diet's decadence, 'the Republic entered into a period of anarchy, paralysis and obscurantism' (Lesnodorski 1959).

Finally, the Diet rules were drastically reformed. In 1764, majority rule was introduced for affairs of minor interest (excluding taxes). In 1791, a new

Constitution established that the Diet could make decisions by majority or by two-thirds qualified-majority on certain issues (such as overthrowing ministers). However, this new period of more efficacious decision making granted by the adoption of new, nonunanimity rules, was short. In 1795, Russia, Prussia and Austria occupied the country and divided Polish state between them (Konopczynski 1930; Davies 1982).

Intergovernmental organizations

Unanimity rule is usually applied in those institutional settings in which the members claim 'sovereignty' and reject any collective decision which is not made with its explicit approval. The councils of two paramount modern international organizations formed by 'sovereign' states are reviewed here, those of the United Nations and the European Community. In both cases, the veto right of every member-state has produced decreasing efficacy in decision making, prompting the replacement of the central or exclusive role of the unanimous council with some alternative institutional scheme.

The Inefficacious United Nations

The relative ineffectiveness of unanimity rule as compared with majority rule can be observed in the two major institutional bodies of the United Nations Organization (UN), the Security Council and the General Assembly, since they work by virtual unanimity and majority rule, respectively. When the UN was created in 1945, the victors of World War II had drawn up a plan to organize a Security Council in which the United States, the Soviet Union, the United Kingdom, France, and China were to be permanently represented. At the first conference of delegates from fifty-one states in San Francisco, these five powers insisted the UN should give them the authority to veto actions of the Security Council. The smaller nations opposed this without success, but they did succeed in adding other UN organs, especially the General Assembly.

The UN Security Council is now formed by the five permanent members mentioned above and ten temporal members elected for two-year terms. Each member has one vote, the five permanent members have veto power, and decisions are made by at least nine votes. The Security Council basically works with the rule of unanimity of its five permanent members (or, in fact, their abstention). It is not difficult for the permanent members to find sufficient support among the temporal members for the proposals they agree upon. The permanent members' power, seen as the probability for them to succeed in approving a common proposal (and ignoring the possibility of abstention), has been calculated to be very close to unanimity, at about 98% (both when the number of temporal members was six and the decision rule was seven votes, and under the above-mentioned rules adopted in 1965 (Brams 1975: 182–91).

The record of annual decisions of the Security Council has remained fairly constant from 1946 to 1990. Its average number of resolutions adopted annually was 89 in the late 1940s and 102 in the late 1980s. During the first forty-five years of the Council, the permanent members of the Council exercised a total of 279 vetoes on sixty-seven different issues (the most conflictive issue being that of the Middle East, with forty-two vetoes). A substantial number of vetoes cast during the Council's early existence were made by the Soviet Union. However, during that same period, a great number of resolutions failed to be adopted because the United States managed to get sufficient support from certain temporal members to defeat the required majority (the so-called 'hidden veto'). The United States also cast a significant number of 'nonhidden' vetoes during the 1980s.

The UN General Assembly includes representatives from every member state (185 in 1999). Each member has one vote and decisions are made by majority. In contrast to the regular performance of the Security Council, the record of the General Assembly during the same period shows a higher degree of efficacy in decision making and a steady increase in the number of resolutions approved each year. The Assembly's record has evolved from an annual average of 117 resolutions adopted in the late 1940s to more than 340 in the 1980s (only nonprocedural but substantive matter resolutions are included in this account). The disparate evolution of the two bodies in their effective decision making is shown in Fig. 3.2 (Marín-Bosch 1987; Patil 1995).

It is of note that the Security Council has a relatively lower degree of efficacy in making decisions despite of its dealing with a high number of issues and the advantage of having much fewer members than the General Assembly. The most important decisions regarding the maintenance of international peace and security have initially been allocated to the Council. But in practice, and due to the inefficacy of its virtual unanimity rule, some questions that have not been resolved in the Council have been added to the General Assembly's agenda. The increasing membership in the UN might have created more difficulties forming majorities among the varied members of the Assembly. But, thanks to the greater efficacy of majority rule, the General Assembly has enlarged the range of its concerns and has steadily increased the number of resolutions adopted.

European Unanimity

When the European Economic Community was founded by the Treaty of Rome in 1957, the Council of Ministers of the initial six member-states—Belgium, France, Germany, Italy, Luxembourg, and the Netherlands—was conceived as its basic institution, although it received initiatives from the European Commission and the Assembly (later transformed into the Parliament). Initially, the six members chose to make decisions in the Council by unanimity, as it would correspond to the 'intergovernmental' or diplomatic model of decision making in international organizations, subject to moving to majority rule on selected subjects in the future. In its first years the European Economic Community, led by the Council's unanimous decision making, was remarkably innovative; it was able to

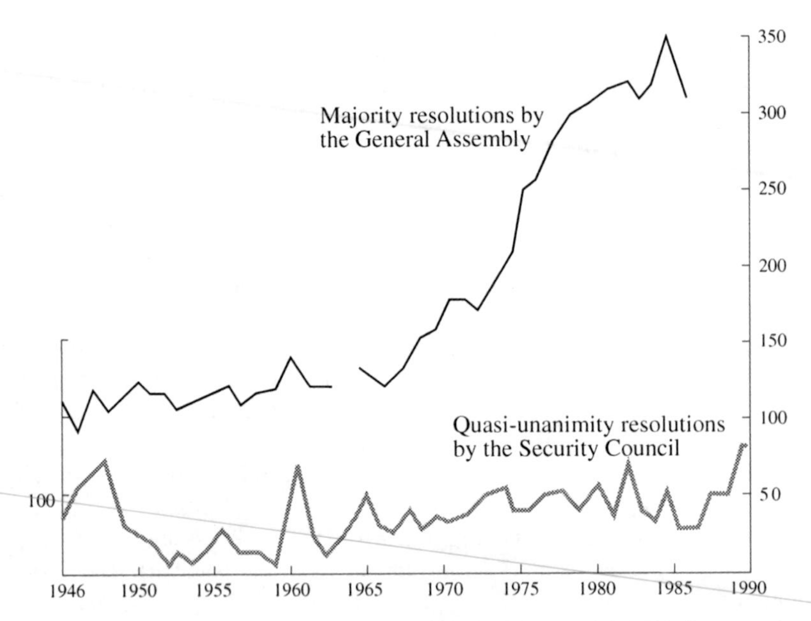

FIG. 3.2. Unanimity and majority resolutions in the United Nations

Note: The left scale shows the number of resolutions approved by the UN Security Council under the veto right of five members. The right scale shows the number of resolutions approved by the UN General Assembly under majority rule. (The 1965 General Assembly is not included because it was a short session)

Source: Marín-Bosh (1987, table 1); Patil (1995).

create an industrial and agricultural common market by lowering customs barriers between its members and to establish common external tariffs favoring trade.

Further development, however, was significantly curbed by the unanimity procedure. In 1963, the French delegation, presided over at that time by General Charles de Gaulle, vetoed Britain's first attempt to join the Community, despite of the fact that negotiations were far advanced. In 1965, when majority rule was due to be introduced for selected matters, the French government began to boycott the Council meetings, provoking the so-called 'empty chair crisis'. This led the members of the Community to agree on the so-called 'Luxembourg compromise' in 1966, a statement in which the right of veto in the Council was formally asserted 'when very important interests were at stake'. For two decades civil servants and ministers of the member-states had to hold lengthy discussions in the Committe of Permanent Representatives and the Council of Ministers until unanimous decisions were reached, leading the Community to a long period of stagnation or 'Eurosclerosis', as it was called at the time. The accession of new members, including Britain in 1973 (after de Gaulle's demise), was a source of new vetoes against further integration, especially during the premiership of

Margaret Thatcher in the early 1980s. Denmark also insisted on the national sovereignty of its institutions, while Germany wanted to preserve the autonomy of its national bank.

In the words of some standard presentations: a 'combination of hostility and inertia . . . impeded the sharing of sovereignty, and stunted Community development between 1965 and 1985' (Pinder 1995); 'decision making was becoming virtually impossible under the practice of unanimity . . . The unit-veto system of the European Council would, in the absence of complex package deals, lead to stalemate on an increasing number of issues. For a major advance in policy integration to take place, these package deals would have had to be so complex that the costs of negotiating them would have become prohibitive' (Keohane and Hoffmann 1990).

Only the adoption of new, nonunanimity decision rules escaping from the limits of the 'intergovernmental' model was capable of furthering more effective decision making. New rules embodied in the Single European Act of 1986 included the 'cooperation procedure', by which the Council shared certain legislation powers with the European Parliament, and the adoption of qualified-majority voting with weighted votes in the Council for most of the decisions concerning completion of the single market program. In the view of the then-President of the European Commission, Jacques Delors, 'the old 'inequality-unanimity-immobility' triangle has been replaced by a new 'equality- majority- dynamism' triangle, the key to success' (Delors 1989).

New revisions of the Community Treaties and further major decisions towards a closer union then became possible, including the creation of a new common currency, the euro, and further enlargements. Specifically, the Maastricht Treaty on the European Union (EU) in 1992 introduced the 'co-decision' procedure in which new legislative powers of the European Parliament were linked to qualified majority voting in the Council of the European Union (as the former Council of Ministers is called since 1993). The 1997 Amsterdam Treaty virtually abolished the cooperation procedure and extended the scope of the co-decision procedure in economic policy making. However, unanimity decisions on important matters are still made at summit meetings of the European Council, composed of the member-states' chief executives, and unanimity in the Council of the European Union is required for decisions on the Common Foreign and Security Policy and on Justice and Home Affairs (Nugent 1994; Crombez 1996; Hayes-Renshaw and Wallace 1997).

Majority

The theological idea of the general will of God, which had been forged within the ancient and early medieval Christian Church, was transformed into the idea of the general will of the citizens in 18th-century French political thought. Accordingly, the praise of unanimity rule, initially associated with God's will, was replaced by certain philosophers' by a similar tribute to majority rule.

For Jean-Jacques Rousseau, the general will was considered to be 'always right' and could be discovered by voting by majority rule. However, Rousseau did not elaborate very much on voting procedures to discover the majority, general will of the people. Rather, he relied upon moral incentives leading citizens to adapt to the general will, however discovered, and substitute it for their particular wills. As an alternative procedure, he suggested resorting to a temporal dictator able to establish or re-establish the people's general will (Rousseau 1762: iv, 2, 6).

Inspired by Rousseau's basic principles regarding the people's general will, Marquis de Condorcet promoted a voting procedure by which the winner should be the alternative preferred by a majority against every other alternative. What is known as Condorcet voting procedure or exhaustive pairwise voting (if multiple rounds of voting between pairs of alternatives are implemented) may be difficult to implement because it requires a complete ordering of preferences, and is highly ineffective in producing an outcome. However, Marquis was eager to counterbalance these drawbacks by asserting the rightness of the outcome when it exists. Voting with multiple majority was conceived as a way to discover the 'best' or the 'correct' decision, one through which 'the people as a whole' could express 'a common will' (Condorcet 1792: 71ff.). A relatively more effective but still difficult variant had been devised in the 13th century by the Catalan philosopher Ramon Llull (1283, ch 24, and 1299).

Majority rule, even with one round of voting by categoric ballot, is certainly much more effective in producing innovative decisions than unanimity rule. In contrast to the latter, majority rule does not give any individual veto power to prevent moves away from the status quo to more efficient outcomes.

Yet, we know from social choice theory that even when a majority winner clearly exists, it may not be socially efficient in terms of social utility. Majority rule is also more vulnerable to instability than unanimity rule. Majority losers can attract sufficient voters' support and overthrow the winner by introducing a relatively lower number of new issues and alternatives than those required to do so under unanimity rule. If appropriate institutional devices exist in order to produce a stable winner, this can be arbitrary and unpredictable from the perspective of voters' preferences, since it will be just one among the many potential winners. The less inclusive the rule, for example, simple majority as compared to qualified-majority rules, the smaller the number of new alternatives and issues that are sufficient to produce instability or unpredictability of the social choice.

Specifically, only in the very simple case of social choice between two

tive can be eliminated at the first round of counting votes (with the first procedure) or at the first round of voting (with the second one). Then the final winner could be beaten by majority by the eliminated alternative if the opportunity to choose between the two were given to the voters.

Only the winner with the Condorcet procedure of voting in a single-dimensional space, that is, the alternative winning by majority against every other alternative on its right or its left, would correspond to the median voter's preference and be socially efficient. By definition, the median voter is always necessary to form a consistent majority in a single dimension. Yet, in a multidimensional space, the Condorcet procedure of voting is highly ineffective (on many occasions an alternative able to win by majority over all the others does not exist) and may be inefficient since the winner may not coincide with the social optimum. Given these disadvantages and the difficulty of voting, the Condorcet procedure has never been used in mass political elections.

Cases: Majority Parliamentary and Presidential Elections

Different cases of mass political elections using the majority principle will be discussed here: (1) Parliamentary elections, including those during the Second Republic of Spain in the 1930s, which used a mixed majoritarian electoral system; the House of Representatives of Australia, with majority-preferential voting; and the National Assembly of France during the fifth Republic, with majority-runoff not always limited to two candidates; (2) Presidential elections with majority-runoff and a second round of voting between the two most voted for candidates in France, producing certain surprising results.

The electoral outcomes analyzed here will show that practical voting procedures based on majority rule do not fulfill such basic requirements of social choice as monotonicity and the independence of irrelevant alternatives. In many of these cases, the social utility of majority winners can be compared unfavorably to likely results with alternative voting rules.

The Spanish Pre-Civil War

Nonmonotonic electoral results in which the loser in popular votes becomes the winner in seats can help to explain high levels of political bipolarization that, under certain circumstances, may lead to revolution, *coup d'état*, and civil war. This was the case in the Spanish Second Republic, which was established in April 1931 in reaction to the previous involvement of the Monarchy in a military dictatorship.

A few weeks after the Republic was proclaimed, the Provisional Government decreed new electoral rules for parliamentary elections to the Cortes. As was explained by the Prime Minister, Manuel Azaña, in a further discussion in Parliament, a majoritarian electoral system was chosen in order to produce a clear parliamentary majority upon 'the indestructible conviction that Republicans and Socialists were the majority of the country'. To the protest that the minorities would be crushed, Azaña, however, acknowledged that he 'didn't know yet whom we are going to crush, or even who will be the crushers and the crushed' (in Mori 1933, vol. XIII: 345ff.).

The electoral system combined majority and plurality rules. About one-seventh of the deputies were elected in ten urban districts and the rest in fifty rural districts with an unfair apportionment of seats. Every elector was given a limited vote for a lower number of candidates than seats to be filled in the district. In each district, the seats were distributed between the two party or coalition lists with higher numbers of votes, respectively called 'the majority' and 'the minority'. If a list was supported by a majority of voters, it was given the proportion of seats they had been allowed to vote for (about 80 per cent). If no list obtained a majority of votes, the most voted list was given 67 per cent of the seats under the proviso that it had obtained at least 20 per cent of votes (40 per cent since 1933). If no list obtained this minimum support, a second round of voting was held. Thus, the second candidacy in votes, the so-called 'the minority', was given only between about 20 and 33 per cent of seats in the district independently of the amount of votes obtained.

It was presumed that these 'majoritarian' rules would favor the fabrication of an oversized, clear parliamentary majority at every election. But unfair district apportionment of seats combined with uneven distribution of votes for different parties across the territory could make the winner in votes a loser in seats.

The electoral system created strong incentives to form large, heterogeneous coalitions of parties at the first round, in the expectation of obtaining the over-representation promised to the most voted list in every district. The numerous, small parties in the broadly populated political center tended very quickly to join either of the two large coalitions with more extreme parties that were formed on the two sides of the left–right spectrum, thus producing increasing bipolarization. The party leaders' strategies to form electoral coalitions were developed asymmetrically on the left and the right and with no continuity from one election to another. In these conditions, the electoral system produced two winners in seats with a minority of votes: in 1933 in favor of the right and in 1936 in favor of the left. On both occasions the opposition to the winner in seats took the form of an armed rebellion.

In the first election in June 1931, the Republican parties (including Left-Republicans, Radical-Socialists, Radicals, and Liberals), running together with the Socialists, obtained a very large, centrist majority over the Monarchists. The Republicans obtained over-representation and a large majority of seats on their own (even without those of the Socialists). In contrast, the disunited Monarchist groups, including Catholics, Agrarians, and Basque and Catalan regionalists, were under-represented.

In the second election in November 1933, the Republican center split into two factions. In contrast to the so-called Left-Republicans and the Radical-Socialists, center-right Republicans, like the Radicals and the Liberals, were now ready to collaborate with the recovered Monarchists.

The center-right Republicans reached irregularly distributed, sometimes informal, pre-electoral agreements in most districts with a reinforced right which was able to organize a new large party, the CEDA, with the Catholics and the Agrarians. Both the candidacies of the center-right and those of the right obtained fewer votes but were given more seats than the more separated center-left and left parties if the latter are counted together, as shown in the electoral results compiled in Table 3.3. Specifically, while the separated center-left and left partes obtained (22 + 14) 36 per cent of votes, they were given only (13 + 8) 21 per cent of seats. This was because the parties on the right half of the spectrum attained narrow majorities or pluralities in a high number of districts and were rewarded with oversized representation. In contrast, the center-left Republicans and the left Socialists, now running separately, became frequent district 'minorities' and were badly affected by the electoral system favoring the larger candidacies.

After the 1933 election, a rather moderate Cabinet led by the center-right

TABLE 3.3. *Bipolarized, nonmonotonic Spanish elections (1931–6)*

1931			1933			1936		
	Votes	Seats		Votes	Seats		Votes	Seats
Republican–Socialist Conjunction	85	89	Left	22	13	Popular Front	46	60
			Center-left	14	8			
			Center-right	30	37	Center-right	23	15
Right	15	11	Right	34	42	National Front	31	25
	100	100		100	100		100	100

Note: Under majoritarian rules, large coalition candidacies obtain higher proportions of seats than votes, in contrast to separated candidacies. Votes and seats are given in percentages. As in other tables in this book, percentages are rounded by the method of greatest remainders: the integers with the greatest remainders are rounded up until they sum 100, and then the other integers are rounded down (following Balinski and Rachev, 1997).

Left: Socialists (PSOE, USC); Communists (PCE); and minor groups.

Center-left: Left-Republicans (AR/IR, UR); Radical-Socialists (RS), Regionals (ERC, ANV, ORGA).

Center-right: Radicals (PRR); Liberals (PP, PC, ASR, DLR, LD); Regionals (PNV, LC); Independents.

Right: Catholics (AN/CEDA); Agrarians (PA); Monarchists (RE, CT); Fascists (FE).

Source: For 1931, Author's calculations with data from Tusell (1982). For 1933, Irwin (1991: 269). For 1936, Linz and de Miguel (1977: 34); Linz (1978: 147–9) with data from Tusell (1971, 1976). More details in Colomer (2000*b*).

Radical party was formed, thanks to the parliamentary support of the right. The largest party in votes and seats, the Catholic CEDA, did not enter the Cabinet directly. Despite this, and in the belief that the CEDA would eventually obtain more influence, in October 1934 the extreme left of the Socialists and the Anarchists organized an armed rebellion to which they were able to attract some center-left Republicans. The rebellion was fought by the army and resulted in more than 1,500 deaths (on both sides) and about 15,000 prisoners.

The election of February 1936 was a kind of revenge. The center-left Republicans and the left Socialists and Communists united and formed the Popular Front. This was basically an electoral coalition that demanded amnesty for the prisoners of the 1934 rebellion and the re-establishment of previous reforms. Significant disagreement on other issues between moderate reformists and revolutionaries was reflected in the programmatic weakness of the coalition.

The center-right Republicans, and especially the Radical party, were badly affected because of their record in the incumbent Cabinet, which underwent several scandals concerning corruption. Some members of the Radical party joined the Popular Front. A new Center party improvised by the incumbent prime minister was not even able to recruit candidates in half the districts. Therefore, this time it was the center-right that was weaker than the large coalition of the center-left and left parties. In addition, the fear of wasting their votes moved a significant number of citizens to vote strategically either for the Popular Front or for the rightist National Front formed by the Catholics, Agrarians, and Monarchists.

The increasing bipolarization promoted by the incentives supplied by the electoral system did not correspond to the degree of bipolarization that could be found among voters' sincere preferences. Using the preferential vote available on the ballot, the citizens gave more votes to the moderate candidates within each coalition or bloc. The center-left Republicans obtained more support than did the Socialists or the Communists in the same lists, while the Catholics received more votes than the Monarchists. In the knowledge of these voters' preferences, party leaders facilitated these choices by placing the more moderate candidates at the top of the lists. Moderate candidates within each of the two blocs were much closer by aligned to each other than to the extreme candidates of their own bloc. In fact, some of the candidates running on opposite coalitions had been members of the same electoral candidacy (or even the same party) just a few years earlier. The more extreme parties obtained almost no support. The Fascists of Falange, with less than 1 per cent of the vote did not obtain representation. The Communist party obtained only 2 per cent of votes, but it was given some over-representation through the coalition lists of the Popular Front (Jackson 1965: 518–25; Linz 1978).

This time it was the Popular Front that obtained fewer votes but was given more seats than the less unified center-right and right parties, if the latter are counted together, as shown in Table 3.3. Specifically, while the separated center-

voter's party can be identified on the basis of ordering the political parties along the left–right axis. In this case, just the noncontroversial location of the Communist party on the left of the Labour party and the sum of their votes is sufficient to identify whether the Labour party or any alternative winner contains the median voter. In precisely fourteen out of twenty-one elections, the median voter's most preferred party was not included in the winning Cabinet (in 1954, 1958, 1961, 1963, 1969, 1972, 1974, 1983, 1984, 1990, 1993, and 1998).

In sum, majority-preferential voting in the election of the lower House of Australia has not suppressed the kind of inconsistencies previously experienced with plurality rule (although it might have given satisfaction to those seeking to undermine the representation of the Labour party). In most elections since 1949, majority-preferential voting has fabricated a winner that does not reflect the wishes of the voters monotonically and can be considered to be socially inefficient.

The French Nonmonotonic National Assembly

Majority rule with a second-round-runoff was introduced in France for the election of the National Assembly by Louis Napoleon after his *coup d'état* in 1851, was enforced most of the time during the Third Republic (1873–1940), and was reintroduced by decree by General Charles de Gaulle after his *coup d'état* in 1958. In the French Fifth Republic, all those candidates who have obtained a certain percentage of votes in the first round of the election can run in the second round. Since the threshold was initially placed at 5 per cent of votes cast, at 10 per cent in 1967, and at 12.5 per cent of registered votes from 1976, the procedure may allow more than two candidates to run in the second round and therefore it does not guarantee a majority winner. But, party strategies have favored desisting in favor of the largest candidate on the same side of the left–right spectrum, in order to avoid the victory of a more distant rival by plurality, thus creating two-candidate races in most districts. 'Divide and win' is, however, still a strategy that certain party leaders have incentives to try.

With this procedure, de Gaulle aimed at producing Gaullist narrow majorities in many districts, many of them filled at the second round, thanks to the elimination or the withdrawal of Conservative and centrist candidates after the first round. In particular, his aim was to cut off the Communists, who had been the first party in votes in the five elections of the Fourth Republic (with an average of over 25 per cent), to a few districts where they would obtain majority or substantial support at the first round.

Accordingly, 'small rural departments were over-represented. Moreover, urban areas were frequently divided and attached to neighboring rural areas in constituencies in which the rural votes would predominate. This was in part the result of the instruction to the prefects that the boundaries should be drawn in such a way as to weaken the Communist Party (but not to discriminate against any other political force). The Ministry of the Interior checked the draft boundaries and sometimes modified them, for De Gaulle was anxious not to penalize leading non-Communist opponents' (Campbell 1965: 129; Cole and Campbell 1989: 92; similar presentations can be found in Macridis and Brown 1960: 238; Williams 1970: 102–3).

The first Assembly election with majority-runoff in 1958 produced effects overwhelmingly oriented in the expected direction. The Gaullist party (at the time called National Union for the Republic, UNR) obtained 21 per cent of votes but was given 43 per cent of seats. The Communist party, which was second in votes (the first in metropolitan France excluding overseas territories), was given only 2 per cent of seats, becoming the sixth largest group in the Assembly. Similar results occurred in the following four elections from 1962, in which the Communists ran second in votes behind the Gaullists, but became third or fourth in seats, and always behind the less-voted for Socialists.

Extreme candidates like the Communists were disadvantaged because many voters of the moderate left turned to other candidates in the second round. But, all the left parties were globally disadvantaged. In 1958, Communists and Socialists together obtained more than 7 million votes and the Gaullists received 4.2 million. But while the first two were given in total only 54 seats, the latter was given 198 seats. Likewise, in 1962, 1967, and 1973, the two major center-right and right parties, the Gaullists and their Republican allies, were together given a majority of seats despite having obtained fewer votes than the Communists and the Socialists, counted together. This created incentives for the left to unite at the first round. By doing so, the Socialists became the first party in votes in 1978, but they were still relegated to the third place in seats behind the Gaullist Rally for the Republic (RPR) and the center-right Union of French Democracy (UDF).

De Gaulle's strategy had been one of bipolarization in the expectation of drawing support from intermediate voters for his nationalist, populist, anti-Communist alternative at the second round. Eventually, the growing electoral support for the nonextreme Socialist Party (PS), mostly at the expense of the Communists, backfired. In 1981, the RPR and the UDF, running separately, obtained together more votes but fewer seats than the PS, which was given a majority of seats in the Assembly. In 1988, the two center-right and right parties mentioned earlier ran together in the first round; their candidacy was the first in votes, but became the second in seats after the Socialists.

In sum, major distortions and nonmonotonic relations between party votes and seats have occurred in eight out of the ten Assembly majority-runoff elections in the French Fifth Republic (in all but those of 1993 and 1997; the 1986 election was held with proportional representation).

From the point of view of social utility, however, the results of the National Assembly elections have been less inefficient than the previously presented distortions may suggest. In a number of cases, the party which was unfairly rewarded with seats by the electoral system was able to form a majority in the Assembly that included the median voter's preference. The median voter was captured by all the center-right parliamentary coalitions and Cabinets in the 1960s and early 1970s, as well as that of the first Socialist parliamentary majority and Cabinet in 1981.

However, on at least two occasions the winner cannot be considered to be socially efficient. In 1978, the most voted PS and its allies of the left gathered together a majority of votes, thus containing the median voter on the left–right axis, but the RPR and the UDF were together given almost two-thirds of seats and formed a Cabinet. In contrast, in 1988 the most voted united coalition of center-right contained the median voter (due to some significant electoral support for the extreme right), but the Socialist party was able to form a parliamentary Cabinet.

Biased Presidents

The rule of majority-runoff was introduced by General de Gaulle not only for the election of the French National Assembly but also for the direct election of himself and the following Presidents of France. It was ratified by referendum in 1962. Majority-runoff has produced more inefficient results in the French presidential elections than in the Assembly elections discussed earlier.

Relatively moderate or popular candidates, such as Georges Pompidou in 1969 (still under the influence of de Gaulle's period), Valéry Giscard d'Estaing in 1974 (broadly), and François Mitterrand in 1981 (narrowly), won with the support of consistent majorities including the political center. Yet in the other three out of the first six elections, the bipolarization enhanced by the electoral system made nonmedian voter's candidates elected Presidents. De Gaulle in 1965 and Mitterrand in 1988 were not the median voter's candidates by relatively narrow margins, and Jacques Chirac was certainly not in 1995. All of them won as a result of the role of irrelevant candidates at the first round.

The electoral results of the first round of the French presidential elections in 1965, 1988, and 1995 are shown in Table 3.4. The median voter's candidate, that is, the only one who would win by majority against any other candidate (or Condorcet winner), is in brackets, while the winner by majority at the second round is in italics. These socially inefficient elections are now submitted to a summary analysis.

The dimension of 'regime support' became highly salient during the electoral campaign of 1965. This was the first direct election of President after de Gaulle's coup against the Fourth Republic and the end of Algeria's war after he granted the colony its independence. The salience of the regime dimension can be captured by the fact that, in the second round, de Gaulle attracted about one-fourth of leftist voters to his policy of political 'stability' and national 'grandeur', while virtually all pro-French Algeria, extreme right voters, joined the left against de Gaulle. On the regime dimension, the Democratic center candidate (supported by the Christian-Democrats and some Radical groups), Jean Lecanuet, occupied an intermediate, potentially more consensual position. (Data on the salience of dimensions during the electoral campaign are given by the polls and analyses of

TABLE 3.4. *French presidential elections with no median-winner (1965–95)*

	1965		1988		1995	
LEFT			Laguiller	2	Laguiller	5
	Barbu	2	Lajoinie	7	Hue	9
			Juquin	2		
	Mitterrand	32	*Mitterrand*	34	Jospin	23
			Waechler	3	Voynet	3
	Marcilhacy	2				
MEDIAN	[Lecanuet]	16	[Barre]	17	[Balladur]	19
	de Gaulle	44	Chirac	20	*Chirac*	20
					de Villiers	5
RIGHT	Tixier	4	Le Pen	15	Le Pen	16
		100		100		100

Note: Numbers are percentages of votes at the first round. The median voter's candidate is between brackets; the winner at the second round is in italics.

For the relative spatial position of the candidates, see Mendès-France and Laumonier (1967); Pierce (1995, tables 4.2 and 8.1).

Fondation Nationale des Sciences Politiques 1967.)

On the left–right dimension, Lecanuet was placed in the middle, between the Socialists and the Communists on one side and the Gaullists and the extreme right on the other, obtaining the support of the median voter in the first round. The bridging role of Lecanuet on the two issue-dimensions is also shown by the fact that, according to both the available polls and post-electoral analysis, in contrast to the consistency of the other candidates' voters' behavior in the two rounds, Lecanuet's voters split: about 60 per cent chose de Gaulle at the second round and about 40 per cent chose Mitterrand (Mendès-France and Laumonier 1967).

There is some additional, perhaps persuasive evidence in support of the hypothesis that had Lecanuet had the chance to be compared with the other candidates by pairs he would have been the majority winner. An expert's summary of a collection of pre-electoral polls states that 'the opinion sector who is favorable to Lecanuet [Democratic Center] bends mostly for an arrangement with the Gaullists, whereas the opinion sector identifying with Mitterrand against de Gaulle wishes, mostly, a rapprochement with the Democratic Center' rather than with the Communists. This may suggest that, first, some relative ideological closeness between most Lecanuet's and de Gaulle's voters, which could form a majority against the left, and, second, the readiness of most leftist voters to support Lecanuet against de Gaulle had the chance been given. Also, post-electoral polls showed large support for the Centrists' balancing role. An absolute majority of voters thought that if the Gaullist Cabinet had needed the support of Lecanuet's party in the Assembly, this would have allowed the latter to control the Cabinet's action (as wished by the left) without the risk of provoking Cabinet instability (against the fears of the Gaullists) (Rossi-Landi 1967). In future years, Lecanuet was seen as embodying 'the nostalgia of centrism, the refusal of two blocs, of manicheism, of bipolarization. Yet this was to fight against the voting rule, against the presidential thing, against the mood of the time' (Duhamel 1983: 73).

The median voter's candidate for President of France in 1988 was the former Prime Minister (under Giscard), economist Raymond Barre, then the candidate of the center-right coalition UDF (formed by Conservative Republicans, Christian-Democrats, Radicals, and Social-Democrats). On the basis of his previous record in government, his party support, and his policy program, Barre was located between two other major candidates, the incumbent Socialist President Mitterrand on his left and the Gaullist Prime Minister Jacques Chirac on his right.

According to some expert analysis of the election, in order to gain access to the second round, the 'Chirac campaign was fundamentally a first-round campaign directed, in spite of its ostensible targeting of Mitterrand, against Raymond Barre' (Gaffney 1989: 134). The latter's entourage, in response, asserted on every occasion that Barre was the best candidate to face Mitterrand in the second round. Finally, the incumbent Mitterrand and the more populist Chirac (the latter in particular criticizing Barre's free market-oriented economic policy proposals) obtained greater support in the first round. As could be expected from the previous insights, the Socialist candidate Mitterrand won in the second round.

It may be interesting to note that, in the honeymoon of his re-election, President Mitterrand immediately dissolved the Assembly and called a new legislative election, but the Socialist party did not obtain an absolute majority. Despite of Barre's defeat, 'Mitterrand's [further] appeals to the center, [his] calls for *ouverture*, and the results of the legislative elections, placed Barre in a nodal position in French politics' (Gaffney 1989: 137).

At the next presidential election in 1995, the retirement of François Mitterrand after fourteen years in the Elysée and the discrediting of the Socialists after a number of scandals concerning corruption gave the center-right a better opportunity to win the Presidency of France. According to the dominant opinion of the time, whichever serious candidate from the mainstream right could make it to the second round was almost certain to win.

After the victory of the center-right in the nonconcurrent Assembly election of 1993 (in one of the few 'monotonic' elections previously analyzed) and the corresponding Cabinet formation, Prime Minister Edouard Balladur was almost taken for granted as the future President by public opinion polls and most of the media. Balladur, a member of the RPR led by Jacques Chirac, was seen as 'reassuring, unpolemical, managerial, thoughtful and competent' in style, as well as 'circumspect, wise, slightly older, moderate in manner, more centrist in outlook and policy proposals' and more pro-European than Chirac (Gaffney 1997, 102–4). Balladur's 'cohabitation' as Prime Minister with President Mitterrand in 1993–5 is widely considered to have been much more effective, smooth, and cooperative than the previous, rather conflictive 'cohabitation' between Mitterrand and Chirac

(1986–8). Balladur was backed by nearly all the center-right UDF and some prominent members of the Gaullist RPR, including all his ministers from both parties, while Chirac had to rely mostly upon his control of the RPR party machine.

We have a very interesting series of opinion polls which were collected and published before the first round of the 1995 election. They include an unusual and enlightening question about the citizen's future electoral choice in different hypotheses of pairs of candidates surviving to the second round. According to the poll results, Balladur would beat Jospin (at least 55 to 45), Balladur would beat Chirac (at least 54 to 46), and Chirac would also beat Jospin although by lower margins (53 to 47, on the same poll). On all the polls Balladur was the Condorcet-winner, the only candidate who would be preferred by an absolute majority of voters to any alternative. (The series of three IFOP polls including this question was completed and compiled in the weekly magazine *L'Express*, 16 February 1995.)

Yet, after a very active campaign for the first round, Jacques Chirac obtained 21 per cent of votes, scarcely one and a half percentage points more than the perhaps too self-confident Balladur, and went to the second round together with the Socialist candidate. Chirac's first round score was barely more than his own in the elections of 1981 and 1988, and far less than any previous successful presidential candidate in France. In the second round, Chirac beat Jospin by almost exactly the margin forecast in the poll mentioned above (53 to 47). Balladur, the median voter's candidate, 'appeared to many after his defeat as the best President France had just lost, a statesperson deprived of office because he did not know the street-fighting rules of party political clashes' (Gaffney 1997: 111).

Interestingly, on two of the three mentioned occasions the nonmedian elected President was eventually forced to 'cohabitate' with a winning median voter's Prime Minister of different ideological orientation, thus creating the opportunity for intermediate, probably more socially efficient compromises between President and Cabinet. This was the case with Mitterrand and Balladur in 1993–5, and with Chirac and Jospin in 1997–2002. In a later section of this book we will discuss how and to what extent cooperation between different winners in separately elected institutions can 'correct' some of the distortions in social utility produced by single-winner electoral rules such as majority-runoff.

Plurality

Plurality (or relative majority) rule is the most effective voting rule. Even with simple categoric ballot, it always produces a winner (except in the case of ties, which is practically negligible in mass elections).

It seems that relative majority rule emerged as an accepted, although not widely noticed, principle for collective decision making in late medieval Europe merely as an expedient resource in response to the failure of unanimity and absolute majority rules to guarantee an outcome. In England, a 1430 statute introduced the majority principle for direct elections in shires. Those with 'the greatest number' of supporters were to be chosen for the Parliament. The sheriff in charge of electoral assemblies could estimate the people's desires either by listening to the shouts of supporters of different candidates or by counting heads and declaring elected those who had more votes than anybody else. Usually, however, the official did not bother to ensure that a candidate was elected by absolute majority, especially if the electoral assembly was a tumultuous affair. 'The rule of the bare majority was thus established' and members of Parliament continued to be elected by relative, not absolute, majority in a system which came to be known as 'first-past-the-post' (Hart 1992: 5).

Even if there might have been similar processes in other countries, the English rule directly expanded to political elections in British colonies and a few imitators in four continents. From the United States, it also expanded to Latin America for direct elections of presidents. While plurality rule might have produced relatively efficient results in simple late medieval societies, it tends to produce highly inefficient results in complex electorates.

With plurality rule, the alternative with the highest number of votes, whatever that number may be, becomes the absolute winner. Thus, the higher the number of alternatives submitted to election, the higher the likelihood that the winner will have only a minority support and the smaller the winning minority can be. However small the potentially winning minority, the general principle of single-winner rules applies and the 'winner-takes-all'.

Plurality rule is most vulnerable to losers' strategies. By introducing relatively few new issues or creating a few new alternatives, plurality losers can alter the winner, thus producing high instability and unpredictability of the outcome in the long run. Plurality rule is more vulnerable to these strategies than majority and qualified-majority rules.

Stated more precisely, plurality winners are highly 'dependent on irrelevant alternatives'. This means that which alternative becomes the plurality winner depends on whether or not some other alternatives are available and can be voted for. Let us assume, for example, that party Left wins against party Right in a pairwise election. Yet, the same voters with the same preferences and voting with the same procedure may make party Right the winner if the choice is presented as being between parties Left, Center, and Right (and a sufficient number of voters prefer Center to Left). The previous loser can become the winner for the same electorate with the same preferences, despite obtaining the same or perhaps even fewer votes than in the previous voting. The new winner depends on the introduction of a new alternative, Center, which does not win (it is 'irrelevant').

Thus, plurality rule works differently with different numbers of parties or candidates. The strategies aimed at altering the number of contenders, such as 'divide and win' and 'merge and win', are highly encouraged in elections by plurality rule. The difference in results that can be produced by plurality rule with different numbers of available alternatives can be most prominently observed by comparing the cases of the United Kingdom, where a three-party system in votes has existed during most of the 20th century, and the United States, which is much closer to a two-party system. As will be documented below, the proportion of parliamentary elections producing socially inefficient winners is higher in the United Kingdom than in the United States.

The plurality winner can be socially efficient if there are only two candidates (then it is equivalent to majority rule) or if a large centrist party is able to maintain its rivals on the left and the right at sufficiently distant positions so as to win the election (as essentially occurred in India with the Congress party, from the country's independence in the late 1940s until the 1980s). However, plurality rule does not usually produce socially efficient winners close to the median voter's preference with more than two parties, as will be observed in the following empirical analyses.

In plurality elections with multiple districts, inconsistent or 'nonmonotonic' relations between votes and seats include the paradox that the loser in popular votes can become the winner in seats. This distortion can be even more striking with plurality rule than with majority rule, as illustrated in Table 3.5. In an election with three (or more) alternatives, even the alternative obtaining the smallest number of votes can become the largest majority alternative in seats. In the example in Table 3.5, an alternative with less than one-third of votes obtains two-thirds of seats against two other more voted alternatives. With plurality rule, the winner may not correspond to the median voter's preference either at the district level or at multidistrict level with relatively high likelihood.

Plurality Procedures

Alternative procedures to categoric ballot based on plurality rule include rank-order count and approval voting. The 18th-century French academician Jean-Charles de Borda invented the first procedure. Rank-order count, also called Borda procedure, requires the voter to order preferences over all the available alternatives giving zero points to the least preferred one, one point to the second-to-least preferred, two points to the next, and so on. The alternative with the highest sum of points becomes the winner (Borda 1784).

Approval voting with plurality rule allows the voters to vote for those alternatives that they consider acceptable, from a minimum of one to a maximum of all minus one. The alternative with the most votes becomes the winner (as formulated by Steven Brams and Peter Fishburn 1983).

Both procedures tend to produce results that are more consistent with voters' preferences and bring about higher social utility than plurality rule

Conservatives against the most-voted Labourites. The alternative victories of Conservatives and Labourites since the 1930s provoked high political instability and heavily biased Cabinets supported by socially extreme minorities. None of the British Cabinets formed after the fifteen elections of the period 1945–97 was supported by the median voter.

In New Zealand, Cabinets in minority among the voters were formed in 65 per cent of the cases, that is, in twenty-two out of thirty-nine elections in the period 1890–1993 (until plurality rule was replaced with proportional representation). In four New Zealand elections, the loser in votes became the winner in seats: in 1911 and 1928 in favor of the Reform party against the most voted Liberals, and in 1978 and 1981 in favor of the National party against the most voted Labourites. These distortions produced by the electoral system reduced the social efficiency of New Zealand Cabinets despite the fact that the country had a very simplified, almost pure two-party system that might have produced majority popular support for the winning party: less than three-fourths of Cabinets in the period 1946–93 were supported by the median voter.

Results are not better in India. Cabinets with a minority of voters' support were formed in 69 per cent of the cases in the period 1952–98 (in nine out of thirteen elections). The median voter supported slightly more than two-thirds of Cabinets thanks to the already mentioned central role played by the Congress party.

The frequency of social biases and nonmonotonic results is somewhat less notorious, although still highly remarkable, in North America. In Canada, fifteen out of thirty-three parliamentary Cabinets in the period 1878–1997 (45 per cent) were supported by a minority of popular votes. On three occasions the loser in votes became the winner in seats: in 1896 in favor of the Liberals against the most-voted Conservatives, and in 1957 and 1979 in favor of the Conservatives against the most-voted Liberals. In the period 1945–97, only seven out of seventeen Cabinets were supported by the median voter.

Finally, plurality rule produced a single-party parliamentary majority with a minority of votes in 30 per cent of elections to the United States House of Representatives, that is, in twenty-six out of eighty-seven cases in the period 1828–1998. Nonmonotonic results have been relatively frequent. On ten occasions, the loser in votes became the winner in seats: in 1846 and 1854 in favor of the Whigs, in the first case against the electoral majority of the Democrats and in the latter producing an absolute majority of seats for the Whigs despite having obtained only 12 per cent of popular support and being the fourth party in votes; in 1836 and 1848 in favor of the Democrats against the most-voted Whigs, in the first case again against an electoral majority for the other party; in 1880 and 1888 in favor of the Republicans against the most-voted Democrats; and in 1858, 1914, 1942, and 1952 in favor of the Democrats against the most-voted Republicans (who obtained an absolute majority of votes in 1942).

Minority White House

The President of the United States is not directly elected by the voters but chosen by the Electoral College, a body which is nowadays elected mostly by plurality rule in fifty-one multimember districts (the states plus the District of Columbia). As in multidistrict parliaments of the British model previously analyzed, the US Presidential Electoral College tends to oversize the representation of the most voted candidate and, with relative frequency, to produce an absolute majority of College electors on the basis of a minority of popular votes. Despite the fact that a simplified party system based on two major alternatives has existed for most of the time since the introduction of competitive presidential elections in 1828, 37 per cent of United States presidents since then, that is, sixteen out of forty-three presidents, have been elected with a minority of popular votes. Minority presidents elected in the period 1828–1996 are the following: the Whig Zachary Taylor in 1848; the Republicans Abraham Lincoln in 1860, Rutherforf Hayes in 1876, James Garfield in 1880, Benjamin Harrison in 1888 and Richard Nixon in 1968; and the Democrats James Polk in 1844, James Buchanan in 1856, Grover Cleveland in 1884 and 1892, Woodrow Wilson in 1912 and 1916, Harry Truman in 1948, John Kennedy in 1960, and William Clinton in 1992 and 1996.

At least on two occasions, the winner in popular votes became the loser in the College and thus in the presidential choice. In 1876, the Governor of New York, Democrat Samuel Tilden, received over a half of the popular votes cast (51 per cent), leading the Republican Rutherford Hayes by more than a quarter million votes or three percentage points. But three disputed Southern states in which fraud and intimidation of black voters was widespread, Louisiana, South Carolina, and Florida, as well as Oregon, sent double sets of College elector returns. The contest was held still in the ashes of the Civil War and, faced with new racial issues, 'at the time probably more people dreaded an armed conflict than had anticipated a like outcome to the secession movement of 1860–61' (Haworth 1906: 168). An Electoral Commission established by Congress and made up of a majority of Republicans, recognized Republican Rutherford Hayes' electors from the above-mentioned states. Hayes was elected by the Electoral College by 185 to 184 votes (Michener 1989: 78–91).

In 1888, Benjamin Harrison obtained less than 48 per cent of votes but was elected president by the Electoral College over the most-voted, Grover Cleveland, who received 49 per cent of votes (a difference of 0.8 percentage points). Harrison ascribed his victory to 'Providence'. (Cleveland was elected with a minority popular support before and after that occasion, as recorded above.)

The 1960 election was particularly controversial. While the Republicans concentrated their support for Richard Nixon, the Democratic candidate John Kennedy ran in parallel to a minor states rights' candidate of his own party, Harry Byrd, who promoted hot positions on racial issues and had significant support in some Southern states. Depending on how the votes of the state of Alabama are

TABLE 3.6. *The United States presidential election (1960)*

	Counting method A		Counting method B		Electoral
	Votes	% votes	Votes	% votes	College
John F. Kennedy	34,220,984	49.48	34,049,976	49.46	303
Richard M. Nixon	34,108,157	49.32	34,108,157	49.55	219
Harry F. Byrd	638,822	0.93	491,527	0.72	15
Others	188,559	0.27	188,559	0.27	—
Total	69,156,522	100.00	68,838,219	100.00	537
					(Majority: 269)

Note: By method A, under which Kennedy is the popular vote winner, the Democratic votes in Alabama are counted twice, both for Kennedy and Byrd. By method B, under which Nixon is the popular vote winner, the Democratic votes in Alabama are divided 5/11 for Kennedy and 6/11 for Byrd, proportionately to the number of electors from the state supporting each candidate in the College.

In the College, Byrd obtained the votes of six unpledged electors from Alabama, the eight from Mississippi, plus one vote by a Republican elector in Oklahoma who defected from Nixon.

Source: Peirce (1968: 101–5). Very close results were previously published in *Congressional Quarterly*, 17 February 1961: 285–8.

counted, the candidate with most votes was either Kennedy, with a plurality of 49.48 per cent of popular votes and an advantage of 0.16 per cent, or Nixon, with a plurality of 49.55 per cent of popular votes and an advantage of 0.09 per cent, as shown in Table 3.6. Without counting Alabama, Nixon won in twenty-six states and Kennedy in twenty-three, but, thanks to having small pluralities in the more populous states, Kennedy was given a majority of electors in the College and was chosen for president.

The Democratic ballot in Alabama included five electors pledged to Kennedy and six unpledged electors who voted for Byrd in the College. Most Democratic voters in the state voted for both pledged and unpledged electors, hence creating a counting problem. If all Democratic votes in Alabama are credited to be for Kennedy, he would have won the national popular vote, but then the electors supporting Byrd would not be credited with any popular votes. Kennedy would have also won if the Democratic votes in Alabama are counted twice, both for Kennedy and for Byrd, but this would make the total number of votes higher than the total number of voters. If, in contrast, the Democratic votes in Alabama are somewhat arbitrarily distributed between Kennedy and Byrd proportionately to the number of electors supporting each candidate, Nixon would have won the national popular vote. Interestingly, the Democratic National Committee used the latter formula in allocating the number of delegate seats each state would have to the following party Convention, implicitly accepting a counting system under which Nixon would have been the popular vote winner. 'In fact, it was impossible to determine exactly what Kennedy's popular vote plurality—if it existed at all—really was' (Peirce 1968: 102).

The result of the election remained uncertain hours after the polls had closed. In the early morning hours of the following day, 9 November 1960, John Kennedy telephoned his father's longtime friend, the Mayor of Chicago, Richard Daley, who told him: 'Mr. President [*sic*], with a little bit of luck, and the help of a few close friends, you're going to carry Illinois'. Later it was discovered that Nixon had won in 93 of the 102 counties of Illinois, but lost at the state level thanks to huge numbers of votes in favor of Kennedy in Cook County (Chicago). Kennedy carried Illinois by a difference of 8,858 votes out of 4,757,409 (less than 0.2 per cent). Speculation of vote fraud was widespread, but electoral recounts bogged down in legal maneuvering on both sides. Even without the twenty-seven electors from Illinois, Kennedy would have had an absolute majority in the College. Yet, with a shift of 4,480 votes in Illinois and 4,491 in Missouri (0.01 per cent of total votes in the United States), Kennedy would not have won the Electoral College (Peirce 1968: 100–10; Reeves 1991: 213–7; on the fraud in Chicago, Kallina 1988; the loser's version in Nixon, 1990: 410–13).

From Plurality- to Majority-Latin-American Presidents

Plurality rule was used to elect the president in virtually every presidential democracy in Latin America until the 1970s. Presidential elections by plurality rule produced biased minority winners leading to political and social turmoil with relatively high frequency. As a consequence, most Latin-American countries moved to more inclusive, alternative rules, mainly majority-runoff, during their processes of redemocratization since the 1970s.

Plurality rule was replaced with majority-runoff or qualified-plurality rule in Ecuador in 1978, El Salvador in 1984, Peru and Guatemala in 1985, Brazil in 1986, Chile in 1989, Colombia in 1991, Argentina in 1973 and again in 1994, the Dominican Republic and Nicaragua in 1995, Uruguay in 1999, and Venezuela in 2000. While Costa Rica retains the rule of 40 per cent since 1936, new variants of rules based on qualified-pluralities were adopted in Argentina, where the Electoral College was replaced with the requirement of either 45 per cent of votes or 40 per cent with 10 percentage points of advantage to the second runner in the first round, and Nicaragua, with the requirement of 45 per cent in the first round. Plurality rule is still used in 2000 in Honduras, Mexico, Panama, and Paraguay. In Bolivia, the second round is transferred to Congress according to rules initially established in 1967. (Majority rule with the second round in Congress was previously used in Mexico in 1864, Cuba in 1901–25 and 1940–6, Costa Rica in 1913–32, and Chile in 1932–70. In Peru a one-third rule with the second round in Congress was enforced between 1933 and 1963, as explained below; Jones 1995*b*, 1997*a*, and the author's direct information. For discussion on the advantages of qualified-plurality rules, Shugart and Carey 1992, appendix A; see also Colomer 1999*b*.)

Table 3.7. Latin-American Presidents (1945–2000)

	Plurality rule		Majority or qualified-plurality rules	
	Majority support	Median voter included		Median voter included
			Costa Rica$_{12}$	83
Argentina$_6$	33	100	Argentina$_4$	100
Brazil$_4$	25	25	Brazil$_3$	67
Chile$_5$	20	20	Chile$_3$	100
Colombia$_{10}$	50	80	Colombia$_2$	50
Ecuador$_5$	0	0	Ecuador$_6$	67
Peru$_4$	25	75	Peru$_3$	100
Uruguay$_{10}$	20	70	Uruguay$_1$	100
Venezuela$_{10}$	40	60		
Election average:	30	59		85
Country average:	27	54		83

Note: Numbers are percentages of elections. Subindices are the number of elections for each country.

Source: Author's own calculations. In order to calculate whether the winner is the median voter's candidate, we need to establish relative candidate's or party's positions regarding the winner, but not necessarily the exact position of the candidates or parties located on the same side of the winner or even less their cardinal positions on the issue space. For this purpose, relative party positions have been found in Nohlen (1993); Mainwaring and Scully (1995); Jones (1995*a*); Huber and Inglehart (1995).

Results for eighty-eight presidential democratic elections in nine Latin American countries in the period 1945–2000 are shown in Table 3.7. Of these elections, fifty-four were decided by simple plurality rule, while whereas thirty-four were decided by majority or qualified-plurality rules in more recent times. The set of countries analyzed here include all of South America except for Bolivia (where all presidents since 1982 have been elected by Congress) and the nondemocratic Paraguay, plus the stably democratic Costa Rica.

A very small proportion of presidents elected with simple plurality rule obtained a majority of popular votes (16 out of 54, or 30 per cent). In only 59 per cent of elections the winning president obtained the support of the median voter.

Relatively more socially efficient results were produced by plurality elections of presidents in those countries with a simplified, almost two-party system, especially in Argentina. In cases like these, there are usually only two main candidates for president and the winner in a single round tends to collect an absolute majority of votes including that of the median voter. Yet two-party systems in pres-idential regimes may provoke relatively high levels of conflict and institutional paralysis when the President's party does not obtain a majority in the Assembly. Divided government with two parties can become an opportunity for confrontational strategies which can be overcome only by difficult unanimity agreements, as will be discussed in the next chapter. In contrast, multiparty Assemblies are more prone to produce viable, nonunanimous majorities able to develop cooperative strategies and to reach compromises with the president. Plurality elections of president in multiparty systems, however, can produce surprising winners dependent on irrelevant alternatives, as will be illustrated below.

Presidential elections with majority or qualified-plurality rules have produced more efficient results than those with simple plurality rules. With qualified plurality rules, no election needed a second round in Costa Rica and Argentina, while only eight out of eighteen elections with majority-runoff needed a second round in the other six countries. In only five of the eight second rounds the winner was different from the plurality front-runner at the first round. This suggests that majority rule induces wider coalition formation already at the first round than plurality-rule.

Precisely, in 85 per cent of the cases (twenty-nine out of thirty-four elections), the winner by majority was the median voter's candidate, in contrast to the 59 per cent of elections by plurality rule previously found. In almost all countries in which the electoral rule was changed—Argentina, Brazil, Chile, Ecuador, Peru, and Uruguay—the proportion of median voter's presidents elected by majority-runoff is higher than with plurality rule in the previous period. Only in the case of Colombia is the new proportion lower, due to the high results obtained in the noncompetitive presidential elections of the previous period of National Front agreement between the two parties (1958–70).

Three Military Coups in Latin America

A very high number of authoritarian regimes in Latin America have resulted either from military coups against weak, minority presidents elected by plurality rule, as will be illustrated below, or from unlimited re-election of a president (as will be discussed in Chapter 4, section 4.1). Presidents are particularly 'weak' or vulnerable when they are chosen with socially biased and minority support, and especially when the majority of voters would prefer an alternative candidate, that is, when the elected is not a Condorcet winner.

Three cases of presidential elections by plurality rule producing nonmedian winners and ending in military coups against 'weak' presidents are analyzed below: those in Peru in 1962–3, Brazil in 1955–60, and Chile in 1970. In the Peruvian case, the military acted merely as self-appointed arbiters: they called a new election under the same rules, which produced a different outcome; in the Brazilian case, the military were innovative electoral rule-makers; and in Chile, they became direct rulers—although, after a period of harsh dictatorship, they introduced new electoral rules too.

One-third of Peruvians

Two presidential elections in Peru in 1962 and 1963 illustrate some of the hazards produced by plurality rule: different candidates can win from the same electorate with the same preferences as a consequence of the role of irrelevant candidates with no expectations of winning.

The voting rule for the election of President of Peru, as established in the Constitution of 1933 (Art. 138), required one-third of valid votes for the candidate to win. If no candidate obtained such a proportion, the election was to be transferred to Congress, which could choose by majority any of the three most-voted candidates.

Three major candidates ran for President of Peru 10 June 1962. On the left, Víctor-Raúl Haya de la Torre was the first viable candidate presented by the American Revolutionary Popular Action (APRA). This populist party, which had a long record of enmity with the Army and had promoted mass action and resistance against a former dictatorship, had not been allowed by the military to run with their own candidates for president in the previous election. Relatively close to Haya were three other minor leftist candidates, respectively supported by the Communists, the Socialists, and the Social-Progressives.

At the center, the major candidate Fernando Belaúnde Terry led the Popular Action Party (PAP). But a close, minor Christian-Democrat, Héctor Cornejo, ran independently. On the right, General Manuel Odría, who had been dictator in 1948–56, led his own candidacy (UNO). (For a longer-term perspective, see Chang 1985; McClintock 1994.)

The three major candidates in 1962 obtained around one-third of votes each (with the former dictator in last position), as shown in Table 3.8. Yet, due to the fragmentation introduced by the minor candidacies, none of the three achieved the required one-third of votes. APRA's Haya de la Torre lacked 5,676 votes (0.33 per cent of total votes). Yet Haya obtained an advantage of only 0.85 per cent of votes over Belaúnde. Had Haya gathered together the votes of any of the other leftist candidates, he would have obtained more than one-third of total votes. But the same threshold would have been achieved by Belaúnde had he collected the votes of the Christian-Democrats. Thus, irrelevant (nonwinning) candidates crucially interfered in the electoral outcome.

TABLE 3.8. *Peruvian presidential elections (1962–3)*

	1962		1963	
LEFT	Pando	2	Samamé	1
	Haya de la Torre	33	Haya de la Torre	34
	Castillo	1		
	Pérez Eldredge	1		
CENTER	Belaúnde	32	*Belaúnde*	39
	Cornejo	3		
RIGHT	Odría	28	Odría	26
		100		100

Note: Numbers are percentages of votes. The winner is shown in italics.

As established by the Constitution, the election of the President of Peru was transferred to Congress in cases in which no party had an absolute majority of seats. Each of the three major candidates was considered to be a potential majority-builder at some moment during the negotiations. However, on 4 July, the chiefs of Armed Forces vetoed Haya's candidacy. Haya in fact, withdrew. In a party meeting two days later he declared: 'We have to acknowledge what was perceivable the day after the election. The APRA party, in the electoral field, cannot be called "party of national majorities" any longer. We should put this honorable title that we have borne for 30 years in the refrigerator and wait to retrieve it in other elections' (Chirinos 1962, 1984: 107).

A military junta took over and annulled the election five weeks after it had been held. Remarkably, they called a new election for the following year 6 June 1963), with no significant persecution of political parties or leaders nor visible repression of political activity in between. The same three major candidates ran again. Eventually, the minor leftist candidates withdrew, while only one new candidate emerged. More decisively, the centrist Belaúnde attained a formal agreement with the Christian-Democrats to jointly support his candidacy. On 13 January 1963, the two party leaders, Belaúnde and Javier Correa, formalized an electoral and, if winning, governmental coalition which came to be known as 'the pact of Salaverry Avenue' (Ramirez y Berrios 1963).

There was increased voter participation this time. Haya obtained a higher number and percentage of votes than he had in the previous election, more than the required one-third. But so did Belaúnde, thanks to the 3 per cent of votes previously given to the Christian-Democrats (as well as a few more from the right and from new voters). In contrast to the previous election, Belaúnde won by plurality.

The following presidential election in Peru was to be held in June 1969. A few months before, the incumbent President Belaúnde experienced increasing unpopularity, the coalition between his party and the Christian-Democrats was broken as a consequence of disagreements in governmental management, and even the rightist candidacy, UNO, had split in two. Again, the APRA party looked as if it had an opportunity to win the presidential election. But a military coup in October 1968 prevented the election and established a ten year dictatorship. The first APRA presidential candidate who was allowed to take office in the history of Peru was Alan García, who won the 1985 election at the first round after plurality rule had been replaced with majority-runoff rule.

Eccentric Brazilians

Several presidents of Brazil elected during the democratic period, which began in 1945, obtained minority popular support. Extreme minority candidates without support of the median voter, that is, no Condorcet winners, alternated in office until a military coup halted the experience in 1964. (For a longer-term perspective, see Lamounier 1994; Mainwaring 1997.)

TABLE 3.9. *Brazilian presidential elections (1945–60)*

	1945		1950		1955		1960	
LEFT	Finza	10						
					Kubitschek + VP Goulart	36	Lott + VP *Goulart*	33
			Vargas	49				
	Dutra	55			Barros	26	Barros	19
			Machado	21	Tavora	30		
							Quadros	48
RIGHT	Gomes	35	Gomes	30				
					Salgado	8		
		100		100		100		100

Note: Numbers are percentages of votes. The winner is shown in italics.

In October 1945, a coup d'etat dismissed dictator Getúlio Vargas and led to the first competitive election with broad suffrage in Brazil. Marshal Enrico Dutra, with last-minute Vargas endorsement, won an absolute majority of popular votes and a majority of seats in Congress. For further presidential and vice-presidential elections, the 1946 Constitution and the 1950 electoral code (Art. 46) established 'the majority principle', which was interpreted by the Superior Electoral Tribunal in 1951 as not requiring more than a plurality of votes. The President and the Vice-President were elected in separated sections of the ballot.

The party system was organized around three basic poles. On the left, the Brazilian Labor Party (PTB), led by Vargas, mobilized voters in industrial and urban areas. The Communist party (which obtained about 10 per cent of votes in the first election) was banned after 1947, and basically supported the PTB candidates in the further process.

At the center, certain Vargas associates created the Social-Democrat party (PSD), with bases in small towns and rural areas, with the aim of joining and moderating the PTB candidates and forming a stable majority. Two minor parties, the Progressive PSP, especially strong in São Paulo, and the Christian-Democrats, also competed for the centrist electorate. On the right, the conservative National Democratic Union (UDN) competed with some minor parties and candidates with similar orientation.

Getúlio Vargas himself ran for President in 1950 with the support of the PTB, the PSP and the Communists, and won with 48.7 per cent of votes, as shown in Table 3.9. Vargas was close but still short of a majority; he was located on an extreme position that did not allow him to be considered the median voter's candidate. Under attack for scandals concerning corruption and the country's economic disaster, and fearing a new military coup, Vargas resigned and committed suicide in August 1954.

For the election of 1955, the pro-Vargas parties supported Juscelino Kubitschek, from an internally divided PSD, for President, and João Goulart, from the leftist PTB, for Vice-President, both also endorsed by the Communists. Kubitschek won with only 35.6 per cent of votes and was certainly not the median voter's candidate. Kubitschek's strength was eroded by the success of the progressive candidacy of Adhemar de Barros, who attracted substantial numbers of Vargas' former voters, especially in São Paulo. Supporters of Juárez Távora, the candidate of the right and some centrist groups, speculated on the victory of his candidate if the irrelevant, independent rightist candidate Plínio Salgado had not ran (Távora and Salgado together collected three percentage points more than the winner).

Kubitschek's inauguration found significant resistance. In September 1954, one month before the election, Congress had defeated a proposal to send the election to the Chamber of Deputies if no candidate received an absolute majority of popular votes and, after the election, the Conservatives argued again before the Superior Electoral Tribunal that the election should be considered invalid for not having produced a majority winner. Prominent political leaders launched accusations of fraud and intimidation and called to establish an 'emergency regime'. A military chief declared that 'to sanction a victory of the minority' and give it 'the enormous sum of power that is concentrated in the hands of the Executive' would be 'an indisputable democratic falsehood'. The progressive Vice-President Cafè Filho experienced heart problems and was replaced as acting President by the chairman of the Chamber of Deputies, Carlos Luz, who was a PSD member but Kubitschek's foe and suspected of conspiring to keep him from taking office. However, a 'preventive' military coup installed Kubistschek as President.

Five years later, in the 1960 election, the candidate for President supported by the pro-Vargas parties, PTB and PSD, obtained still less support than on previous occasions, again in competition with the irrelevant Barros. The winner was Jãnio Quadros, the candidate of the now united right and center-right, with 48.3 per cent of votes. Quadros was close but still short of a majority; he was located on the opposite extreme position, also without the median voter's support. Moreover, the winning Vice-President was João Goulart, the leftist candidate, thanks to a significant number of split-ticket votes. First, President Quadros appointed a national 'concentration Cabinet', with members from the right and the left. But, surprisingly, he undertook a number of leftist policy initiatives, including approaching the new revolutionary Cuban regime, and attempted ruling without Congress.

In August 1961, Quadros resigned eight months after his inauguration, apparently on miscalculation to provoke a fervor of popular support, which would have allowed him to take exclusive powers. According to constitutional provisions, he was replaced by Vice-President João Goulart, who became the most extreme minority President since 1945. The military leaders accepted the appointment of the new president only by depriving the office of significant powers and imposing a parliamentary regime (one of the rare experiences of parliamentarism in

Latin America in the 20th century). However, Goulart regained full presidential powers at a plebiscite in January 1963. A few months later, he formed a Cabinet with the exclusive support of the PTB-PSD parties. Goulart's request for a state of siege was refused by Congress, but he launched a series of mass demonstrations that were widely interpreted as an attempt to override the established institutional mechanisms. In March 1964, the PSD officially split from the government, which was left exclusively in the hands of the minority PTB. Three weeks later, a military coup disbanded the elected leaders (Skidmore 1967; Dulles 1970; Stepan 1971, 1978).

The military Junta established in Brazil in 1964 experimented with some new rules, not with much success. It curbed Congress powers, while keeping regular legislative, state governorships, and mayoral offices elections. The traditional political parties were replaced with two parties formed from those above and tried to represent both the right and the left. Presidential elections were allocated to Congress, with the requirement of absolute majority in two rounds and only plurality in the third round. The last indirect presidential election was held in 1985, but the opposition demands of *diretas-jà* (direct elections now) was widely associated to effective democratization and legally established in 1986. The following democratic presidential elections used majority-runoff rule.

The Chilean Way to *Coup d'État*

As with other presidents elected by plurality rule, the 1970 Chilean winner, Salvador Allende, was dependent on irrelevant alternatives. The median voter was not included among his supporters. Further confrontational strategies between the extreme, minority winner and a potential alternative majority led to social conflict, *coup d'état*, and military dictatorship. (For an extensive analysis, see Valenzuela 1976, 1978, 1994.)

The Chilean Constitution of 1925, which was continuously enforced from 1932, established that the President should be elected by absolute majority of popular votes. Had no candidate obtained a majority support, the President would be chosen by Congress from between the two candidates with the highest number of votes. In the elections of 1946, 1952, and 1958, Congress always elected the plurality-winning candidate, even if the parties that supported the president in the popular election did not have a parliamentary majority.

Plurality rule was thus not legally established in Chile (in contrast to most other Latin-American countries), but it was stringently enforced by political parties. Usually, the second candidate in votes conceded the election in favor of the plurality winner without waiting for the decision of Congress. In 1964, the Christian-Democratic candidate formally declared, even before the election, that he would not accept the presidency if he were not the candidate with the most popular votes.

There is remarkable evidence that the basic distribution of Chilean voters' preferences, as can be located on left, center, and right positions of the ideolog-

TABLE 3.10. *Chilean presidential elections (1958–70)*

	1958		1964		1970	
LEFT	Allende	29	Allende	39	*Allende*	37
	Zamorano	3				
	Bossy	15	Duran	5		
MEDIAN	Frei	21	*Frei*	56	Tomic	28
RIGHT	*Alessandri*	32			Alessandri	35
		100		100		100

Note: Numbers are percentages of votes. The winner is shown in italics.

ical spectrum, did not change significantly throughout the 1950s and the 1960s (Prothro and Chaparro 1976). In contrast, drastic changes were introduced in the formation of party coalitions in the elections of the same period.

The results of presidential elections in Chile since 1958, the year when a legal reform abolished local party pacts and induced a more consistent organization of the national party system on the left–right axis, are shown in Table 3.10. As can be seen, the right-wing candidate, Jorge Alessandri (supported by the Conservative and the Liberal parties, lately merged into the National party), won in 1958 with less than a third of popular votes. Alessandri was less than three percentage points ahead of Salvador Allende, the candidate of the united left of Socialists and Communists. As was noted at the time, if the irrelevant, independent leftist candid-ate, Antonio Zamorano, a defrocked priest known as *el cura de Catapilco* (the priest of the little village of that name), had not entered the contest and obtained more than 3 per cent of votes, Allende would probably have won. On the other hand, Alessandri would probably also have won in a second round by majority. Neither of the two top minority runners (Alessandri and Allende), however, was a Condorcet winner or the median voter's candidate since each of them would have been defeated by the intermediate candidate, Eduardo Frei, in pairwise contests.

Fearing victory of the left, the incumbent President's party did not present a candidate of its own in 1964. The National party decided to endorse the centrist candidate, Frei, who, facing an asymmetric number of rivals, obtained an absolute majority of votes from the center and the right. With 56 per cent of popular support, Frei was certainly the median voter's candidate. Exceptional for Chile's modern history, President Frei's party also obtained an absolute majority of seats in Congress in the election held shortly after his inauguration.

Encouraged by his majority support in both the presidential and congressional elections, Frei introduced a constitutional reform reinforcing the president's powers (regarding the president's legislative veto, reserved domains, and the power to call referendums). The unbalanced relation of powers between the

President and Congress created by this reform did not help to build further compromises between the two institutions but rather fostered interinstitutional conflict.

Several attempts at replacing plurality rule with majority rule for the election of President failed: both when the proposal was introduced by Alessandri in the final period of his mandate, by Frei shortly after his election, and by several members of Congress during the discussion of the just-mentioned successful constitutional reform. In each case, the reform of the electoral rule was blocked by minority yet sufficiently large parties with expectations of winning by plurality. The left and the Christians rejected Alessandri's proposal for majority rule in 1964, and the National party prevented the reform during further discussions in 1964 and 1969.

For the election of November 1970, the right again presented its own candidate, Alessandri. National party leaders were troubled by the unusually high concentration of power in the hands of the incumbent President, as well as by the recent leftist ideological turn of the Christian-Democrats, especially after the choice of their new candidate, Radomiro Tomic. The right-wing leaders expected that Alessandri would obtain greater popular support than the centrist candidate (as he certainly did). The other intermediate party, the Radicals, split and the fraction keeping the party name decided, in contrast to previous elections, not to present a candidate of its own but rather to join the Socialists and the Communists (as well as other minor groups) in support of the leftist candidacy of Allende. Facing now two separate candidacies of the center and the right and without rivals on the left side of the spectrum, this time Allende won. Remarkably, in 1970, Allende obtained a smaller proportion of votes, less than 37 per cent, than he had in 1964 (and smaller than the sum of votes the parties supporting him now had obtained in separate candidacies in 1958).

In contrast to previous presidents and the other candidates, Allende was the last preference of a majority of voters. Most voters who supported the Christian-Democratic party's and the National party's candidates would have preferred each other's candidate instead of the leftist one. Even among voters of the 'lower socioeconomic group', according to the polls, Allende was as much rejected as Alessandri (Prothro and Chaparro 1976: 88; Valenzuela 1978: 42). In a majority voting against either candidate, Allende would certainly have been the loser, that is, he was the Condorcet loser.

However, he was elected by Congress with the votes of the Christian-Democrats, together with those of his own supporting parties. In a secret meeting before the election, Allende and Tomic had agreed that the plurality winner would be recognized by the other candidate if he obtained an advantage of at least 30,000 votes over the second most-voted candidate (Fontaine 1972: 66). The agreed sufficient difference was roughly equivalent to 1 per cent of votes and, in face, Allende surpassed Alessandri by slightly more than 39,000 votes, that is, by about 1.3 per cent. With the decision to confirm Allende as the plurality-winning president, the Christian-Democrats expected to become the leading opposition party against the leftist government, a strategy that was considered preferable in the medium term than joining the rightist party's potentially winning candidate as a minor, subordinate partner. As an exchange for the Christian-Democratic votes, Allende agreed to support a constitutional amendment or 'Statute of Guarantees' requiring him to respect civil liberties, elections, and freedom of the press. Despite of the orders from US President, Richard Nixon, to the CIA, US agents were unable to bribe Christian-Democratic congressmen or military leaders to prevent Allende's election by Congress.

The Allende government rapidly undertook a number of radical reforms, including the nationalization of farms and factories and a wide redistribution policy. A negative majority was soon formed. Whereas the reinforced President's legal powers had eroded the traditional spaces of interinstitutional accommodation, a new cooperation between the opposition parties in Congress developed and combined with street demonstrations and strikes against the government. In September 1973, in the midst of full political deadlock, a military coup initially supported by the right and most Christian-Democrats established a dictatorship which lasted for more than fifteen years. About 3,000 persons were persecuted and killed in the first few months after the *coup*. The next democratic presidential election took place in 1989, using majority-runoff rule. The Christian-Democratic candidate, with the support of the Socialists, won the Presidency in the first round.

3.2. MULTIPLE-WINNER RULES

Multiple-winner outcomes can be attained in two stages: (1) elections with proportional representation; and (2) the formation of assembly multiparty coalitions. As will be discussed in the following pages, the outcomes of this two-stage process (the Assembly or Cabinet positions and the corresponding public policies) tend to be more inclusive, moderate, and stable than the typical outcomes obtained with single-winner rules.

Multiple-winner rules reinforce themselves. By fostering the emergence, strength, and survival of multiple political actors, they obtain broad support from the corresponding actors and tend to become equilibrium solutions. Multiple-winner rules will be evaluated here for the social efficiency of their outcomes.

Proportional Representation

The principle of proportional representation in political bodies has been enunciated on several occasions since the late 18th century, but it was not linked to practical formulas for its implementation for quite a long time. One of the first statements in favor of proportional political representation can be attributed to Honoré Gabriel Riqueti, Count De Mirabeau, in his address to the provincial Estate (Assembly) of Provence on 30 January 1789, that is, in the process of electing the Estates-General which would trigger the Revolution in France.

According to Mirabeau, 'the Estates-General are to the nation what a chart is to its physical configuration; in all its parts, and as a whole, the copy should at all times have the same proportions as the original' (author's translation from Mirabeau 1789, vol. 1: 7). In Mirabeau's view, representation of all parts should prevent the two dominant Estates, the aristocracy and the clergy, from prevailing over the whole nation. His requirements for an acceptable government included universal suffrage, proportional representation, and the power of the representatives to make effective decision—in other words, the basic components of a democratic social choice that were identified in the introduction to this book.

In a lesser known passage of the same speech, Mirabeau stated precisely that 'the nation is not there [in the Estates] if those who call themselves its representatives have not been chosen in free and individual elections, if the representatives of groups of equal importance are not equal numerically and in voting power'. For Mirabeau, was not only a question of faithful representation of society based upon equal voting rights of individual members of the three estates and fair apportionment, but also a question of obtaining socially efficient outcomes. 'In order to know the will of a nation, the votes must be collected in such a way so as to prevent the mistake of taking the will of an estate for one other, or the particular will of certain individuals for the general will' (idem: 7–8).

Within the British utilitarian tradition, proportional representation was promoted with the aim of producing a broader distribution of political satisfaction among different groups in the society than majority rule could produce. John Stuart Mill, most prominently, attacked majoritarian rules because they produce 'class legislation' and 'class rule'. According to Mill, the winner in plurality-rule parliamentary regimes with two stages in the process of decision making (popular elections and Cabinet formation in Parliament), is actually 'a majority of the majority, who may be, and often are, but a minority of the whole'.

In contrast, proportional representation would give power to the majority and the minorities, to all 'interests' or 'classes', in the aim of giving every group 'protection against the class legislation of others without claiming the power to exercise it in their own'. For Mill, a good government should prevent the exclusive rule of a single winning group and favor multiple winners' power-sharing. For this aim, proportional representation was the right institutional choice because it 'makes it impossible for partial interests to have the command of the tribunal, but it ensures them advocates' (Mill 1861, ch. 7).

More formally enunciated, the principles of proportional representation can be found in the work of several 19th-century mathematicians. Specifically, in Charles L. Dodgson's (Lewis Carroll) presentation, desirable principles include that 'the number of unrepresented electors should be as small as possible', and that 'the proportions of political parties in the House should be, as nearly as possible, the same as in the whole body of electors' (1884, in McLean and Urken 1995: 41–54, 300).

As suggested, some early promoters of proportional representation used images like 'chart', 'map', 'picture', 'portrait', 'mirror' 'looking-glass'. (For a collection of quotations using these types of metaphors, see Pitkin 1967: 60ff). The most prominent authors, however, did not intend a mere reproduction of the complexity of society within political institutions. As explicitly stated by the authors quoted above and clearly suggested by the context in which these principles were formulated, they aimed at preventing the maintenance or emergence of a single, absolute winner—the dominant estates, a class rule—and the exclusion of significant groups from the institutional process, in favor of better social choices. Some authors tried to make room for the middle and lower classes previously excluded by aristocratic domination; others wished to prevent the establishment of exclusive working-class rule. Inclusiveness in decision making and power-sharing was expected to produce more satisfactory results. In other words, proportional representation was not only promoted for obtaining fair electoral results as an end in itself, but with the aim of producing political outcomes with greater social utility than more exclusive rules. Lewis Carroll's clever quotation that begins the chapter, describing a race in which 'everybody wins and all must have prizes', makes this point in a flash.

Parallel to the enunciation of these general principles, several mathematical formulas of proportional representation were invented in the United States at the end of the 18th century, although they were not used then for allocating seats to different parties or groups. As stated in the United States Constitution (Article 1, Section 2): 'Representation and direct taxes shall be apportioned among the several States which may be included in this Union according to their respective numbers' of citizens. Several formulas of 'fair apportionment' were thus conceived with the aim of allocating House representatives to the states, although they were going to be elected by plurality rule.

The basic mathematical formulas which were to be used in political elections elsewhere beginning in the late 19th century were invented by the Founding Fathers of the American Constitution. Some formulas divide the number of citizens (or votes) by a series of divisors and allocate seats to the largest quotients obtained. These include Thomas Jefferson's proposal in 1791, which was reinvented by Belgian lawyer Victor d'Hondt for proportional elections in 1878 and (with different counting procedures producing the same result) is also known as Hagenbach-Bischoff, as well as US Senator Daniel Webster's proposal in 1832, which was reinvented by the French mathematician André Sainte-Laguë in 1910. Other formulas allocate seats on the basis of a quota (of citizens or votes) and the greatest remainders, including in particular Alexander Hamilton's proposal in 1792, which was reinvented, quite independently, by English schoolmaster Thomas Wright Hill in 1821, Danish mathematician and politician Carl C. G. Andrae in 1855, and English lawyer Thomas Hare in 1857 (and usually known as The Hare quota). (Other formulas were proposed by former President John Quincy Adams, mathematician James Dean, and statistician Joseph A. Hill; discussants include George Washington and James Madison; see Balinski and Young 1982.)

Pluralistic Voting Procedures

Proportional representation requires multimember districts. But it can be implemented with different ballots in order to select either individual candidates or party lists. The following paragraphs review several pluralistic voting procedures: multimember elections with majoritarian formulas, single transferable vote, and party lists.

Multimember, Majority Elections

When a connection had not yet been established between the principles of proportional representation and the corresponding mathematical formulas, other devices aimed at preserving some minority representation in elections using majoritarian rules were introduced in a number of countries. Limitedly pluralistic, nonproportional procedures include cumulative vote and limited vote.

Cumulative vote allows each voter to concentrate several votes on a single candidate or distribute them among several candidates. In accord with the utilitarian aim of maximizing the sum of individual utilities, this procedure enables voters to express the intensity of their preferences. Yet it is highly vulnerable to strategic vote. By concentrating insincere votes on the most preferred candidate, voters tend to choose in cumulative voting as they would with categoric ballot. Cumulative vote was used in certain elections in Chile and in the South African province of Cape of Good Hope in the 19th century and for the State Assembly of Illinois until 1980.

Limited vote allows each voter to vote for fewer candidates than the number of representatives which are to be elected in the district. Limited vote was used for electing a few members of the British House of Commons in 1886–90, the local Councils of Boston and Philadelphia, as well as the national parliaments of Spain, Portugal, and some Latin-

American countries in the late 19th century. A variant called single nontransferable vote (SNTV), which gives each voter only one vote, was used in Japan after World War II until 1994. (For the effects of multimember districts with limited vote, see Carroll as discussed by Black 1996; for the Japanese SNTV, see Lijphart, López-Pintor, and Sone 1986; Cox 1997: 100–8, 240–50.)

Single Transferable Vote

This voting procedure requires each voter to rank individual candidates in the ballot. It is an eliminatory method similar to the Australian alternative vote previously discussed, but it is applied to multimember districts. Seats are allocated to candidates who have obtained a quota of votes (usually the Droop quota) while the remaining votes are transferred to the following candidates in voters' ordinal preferences.

Single transferable vote (STV) allows a moderate pluralistic representation (Katz 1984). Yet, like all quota systems, STV may produce nonmonotonic results (Doron and Kronik 1977). It does not prevent strategic voting since it would be possible for some voters to induce an early elimination of less desired candidates in the first counts in order to favor the survival of less popular candidates in further rounds of counting (Brams and Fishburn, 1983). However, the computational effort that would be required to take advantage of this possibility is so enormous, even if there is complete information on voters' preferences, that it would be extremely difficult to pull off a strategic vote. Thus, STV can be considered to be strongly resistant to manipulation (Bartholdi and Orlin 1991).

STV was first invented by Thomas W. Hill in 1821 and first used in local elections in the small colonial town of Adelaide (South Australia) in 1839. On a second, unrelated occasion, STV was devised by Swiss mathematician and Minister of Finances (and later Prime Minister) Carl Andrae and used for the first time in national parliamentary elections in Denmark between 1856 and 1863. Thomas Hare (who was perhaps influenced by Jeremy Bentham, according to a suggestion in Hart 1992: 29) was able to present the procedure in a much more precise manner in 1857 and 1859. He gained fame as its inventor, despite its earlier authors, thanks in great part to public praise of the system by John Stuart Mill and a subsequent opinion campaign and parliamentary proposals.

STV has been used in local elections in former British colonies, including Canada, Tasmania, and South Africa. In the United States, it extended from the town of Ashtabula, Ohio, in 1915 to twenty-two city councils including Boulder, Sacramento, Cleveland, and Cincinatti in the 1920s, and to New York City between 1937 and 1947, where it created the occasion for the election of a few black and Communist aldermen for first time in the city's history. It is nowadays used for the election of the city council and school committee of Cambridge, Massachusetts, and New York City school boards. Single transferable vote is used for national parliamentary elections in the British-inspired political systems of Ireland and Malta since 1920, and for the Australian Senate since 1949; as well as in Estonia in 1992 (at the induction of political scientist Rein Taagepera) (Hoag and Hallet 1926; Weaver 1984, 1986; Mair 1986; Tideman 1995; and author's information).

Party Lists

The principle of proportional representation encourages many parties or candidates to run separately according to their own profile, that is, not to withdraw or merge. The strategy of entering the race independently can be based on the expectation that every candidacy can obtain a sufficient number of votes to be represented in the Assembly and have some further influence in legislation and Cabinet formation. Pure proportional representation is not manipulable because is not a 'single-valued' decision procedure, according to social choice theory. In contrast to single-winner rules, such as plurality or majority rules, proportional representation is not vulnerable to strategies, such as manipulation of the agenda by introducing new alternatives (traditionally known as 'divide and win' tactics), or giving salience to different issue-dimensions (see Nurmi 1987).

In principle, proportional representation also encourages sincere voting by the citizens, since voters can expect that their political preferences will be satisfied to the extent that they coincide with those of other citizens. With a high number of parties or candidates running and sincere votes on the part of citizens according to their preferences, proportional representation usually creates Assemblies in which no party has an absolute majority of seats.

There are, however, some specific effects produced by the different proportional representation formulas. Quota formulas can produce some nonmonotonic results from somewhat unusual combinations of numbers such that an increase in the number of votes (or citizens) may produce a decrease in the number of seats. (This is the 'Alabama paradox' that was discovered on the occasion of allocating US House seats to the states.)

Both the quota formulas and the Webster-Sainte Laguë formula encourage party fragmentation and even the independent running of individual candidates from the same party because it may give a coalition fewer seats than its partners can obtain separately. Under this institutional framework, if different parties are created by political entrepreneurs, they can survive separately; if the initial situation is dominated by a few parties, some of their candidates can find incentives to split from the party and run on their own. In contrast, the Jefferson-d'Hondt formula favors larger parties and thus encourages the formation of electoral coalitions. (Some discussion of the incentives for fragmentation and coalition can be found in Balinski and Young 1982: 87–93. An extreme example of party fragmentation induced by a quota formula of proportional representation is in Colombia; Cox and Shugart 1995; the consequent electoral reform introducing the d'Hondt formula was discussed and supported by international experts see Valenzuela 1999.)

For all the formulas, the higher the number of seats in the district, or district 'magnitude', the more proportional representation is obtained. Specifically, there is an inverse relation between the 'effective threshold' of votes needed by a party to obtain seats and the district magnitude. (Lijphart 1994*a*; Taagepera 1998). The degree of proportionality of electoral results can be measured with several indices comparing proportions of votes and proportions of seats for each party (see the discussion in Gallagher 1991).

Thus, manipulation may appear in elections by proportional representation to the extent that a small district magnitude tends to exclude some parties and produce significant deviations from proportionality, but not when the allocation of seats approaches full proportionality to each party-vote share. (For other formal analyses of the effects of electoral formulas of proportional representation, see Taagepera and Shugart 1989; and for an empirical survey, see Lijphart, 1994*a*. A few examples of strategic behavior in systems with quota formulas or small district magnitude are identified in Cox 1997: 108–22.)

Proportional representation on the basis of votes given to different party lists was proposed by Socialist Victor Considerant as early as 1834. His influence on the Swiss writer Morin in the 1860s eventually led to the adoption of proportional representation in the Swiss canton of Ticino in 1891 and in other cantons in the following years. An unrelated publication on the topic was Thomas Gilpin's pamphlet printed in Philadelphia in 1844 (and reprinted in the *Annals of the American Academy of Political and Social Sciences* in 1896).

The Argentinean provinces of Buenos Aires in 1873 and Mendoza in 1895 early on adopted systems of proportional representation based on party lists. Proportional representation was also adopted for party-list national parliamentary elections in Serbia in 1899 (after being used for local elections in 1888), Belgium in 1899, Finland in 1906, Cuba in 1908, Sweden in 1909, the Portuguese districts of Lisbon and Oporto in 1911, Bulgaria in 1911, and Russia in 1916. In the years 1918–20, immediately after World War I and the dissolution of the German, Austrian, and Russian Empires, all the constituent Assemblies which met in the newly created states decided on a list system of proportional representation for national elections, including Austria, Germany, Italy, the Netherlands, Norway, Poland, Romania, Switzerland; the micro-states of Luxembourg,

San Marino, Liechestein, and Danzig; Estonia, Latvia, and Lithuania, as well as Far Eastern Republic (Siberia), Armenia, and Georgia before being annexed to the Soviet Union. Hungary adopted the same principles in 1925 (Hoag and Hallet 1926; Carstairs, 1980).

Most newer democracies established in Western Europe at the end of World War II, and in Southern Europe, Latin America, and Eastern Europe during the last quarter of the 20th century also adopted party-list systems of proportional representation for national political elections (as will be discussed in Chapter 5).

Nearing the year 2000, the Hare quota formula is being used in Bolivia, Colombia, Costa Rica, Germany, and the proportional portion of Lithuania. The d'Hondt (or Hagenbach-Bishoff) formula is used in the Czech Republic, Finland, Iceland, Israel, the Netherlands, Portugal, Slovakia, Spain, Switzerland, and the proportional portions of Hungary and Italy, as well as in Argentina, Brazil, Chile, Ecuador, Peru, Uruguay, and Venezuela. Modified Sainte-Laguë formulas are used in Denmark, Norway, and Sweden. Austria and Belgium combine Hare and d'Hondt formulas.

Multiparty Coalitions

As a result of both partys' and voters' strategies, proportional representation tends to produce multiple winners. Proportional representation does not, however, produce outcomes as directly as do plurality or majority rules. When the latter formulas are used in mass political elections, a single winner (either a parliamentary party led by a candidate for premier or a president) is usually known a few hours after voting. In contrast, parliamentary elections with proportional representation transfer the decision to an additional institutional stage. There, actors can negotiate to form or support a Cabinet.

A series of analytical and empirical studies of Cabinet formation in parliamentary regimes shows that the assumption that parties keep their ideological connectedness when they form coalitions performs better than alternative assumptions, such as those based merely on the size of the coalitions. In parliamentary negotiations, political parties tend to maintain relative policy-ideological positions that are consistent with their relative positions during the previous electoral campaign. They prefer coalition partners located at neighboring positions in the policy-ideology space to those at more distant locations. Within this policy-ideology condition, parties tend to form coalitions without superfluous partners. (For the concept of minimum connected winning coalitions, see Axelrod 1970. For comparative analyses, see Laver and Schofield 1990; Laver and Budge 1992; Laver and Shepsle 1996.)

Minority Cabinets in parliamentary regimes can also be largely explained by the assumption that political parties that might form an alternative majority in parliament on the basis of their numbers of seats abstain from doing so if they occupy too distant policy-ideological positions or are not connected on the left–right axis. Then, a centrist party (or coalition) containing the median seat, even if it is not supported by a majority of seats, can survive noncredible threats to overthrow it from ideologically separate parties on its left and right. (Strom 1990.)

A similar assumption regarding the ideological connectedness of multiparty coalitions (but not regarding the size of the coalitions) can be made for Assemblies in presidential regimes and other nonparliamentary institutional settings in which multiparty majorities are formed. (For the concept of connected winning coalitions, see Colomer 1996*d*; Colomer and Hosli 1997.)

If party policy-ideology positions matter, centrist parties—and especially the party containing the median seat—can be relatively advantaged in parliamentary negotiations to form a majority. Let us remember once again that the median is defined as the position having no more than half of the seats on both its right and left. If parties keep their ideological connectedness on the left–right scale when they form a majority coalition to appoint or support a Cabinet, which is to say if every party is only ready to form a coalition with adjacent parties, then the party containing the median seat is always a necessary partner in gathering a majority or allowing a minority Cabinet to survive. If parliamentary representation is proportional to different voters' preference groups, the median seat corresponds to the median voters' preference. We thus find the paradoxical result that interactions of parties that give prominence to their policy and ideological positions in choosing partners tend to produce ideologically moderate outcomes. This differs from results in elections with alternative formulas, such as plurality rule, in which it is possible to form a majority in parliament without including the position of the median voter.

In order to illustrate this result, Fig. 3.3 compares hypothetical majority coalitions formed from proportional representation, which always include the median voter, and more biased plurality winners. A plurality winner is operationalized as the largest plurality short of a majority. In the following examples, the plurality winners are supported by 40–44 per cent of popular votes (proportions that are quite close to the typical single-party plurality Cabinet in the United Kingdom).

For a distribution of five preferences with roughly the same proportion of voters in a single dimension, only half of the coalitions encompassing the largest plurality (2/5, 40 per cent) include the median voter. For seven preferences, the proportion of coalitions encompassing the largest plurality (3/7, 43 per cent) that include the median voter rises to 60 per cent, and

as the average position of all the parties in the Cabinet, weighted by their proportion of seats. Results also hold with respect to the position of the median party in the Cabinet coalition. Similar results are found regarding the mean voter. (The sample reported here includes Australia, New Zealand, the United Kingdom, France, Belgium, Denmark, Germany, Ireland, Italy, the Netherlands, Spain, and Sweden in the period 1968–87; Huber and Powell 1994.)

Cases: Efficient Multiparty Cabinets

Socially efficient outcomes produced by proportional representation and multiparty coalitions will be illustrated with several cases of Cabinet formation in parliamentary regimes in Western Europe. The following survey includes two cases that have obtained rather bad scores in certain received opinion, especially for their high levels of ministerial instability: the French Fourth Republic (1945–58) and the Italian First Republic (1945–93). Two cases with a higher reputation in achieving governance are also discussed: the Dutch parliamentary Monarchy (here surveyed for the period since 1945) and the German Federal Republic established in 1949. The following analysis of these countries' institutional formulas will focus upon the inclusiveness of the political representation they promote and the stability and social efficiency of the resulting Cabinet positions and policy outcomes. From this point of view, the performance of proportional representation and the corresponding multiparty coalitions obtains a clearly positive evaluation for the four countries mentioned.

The French Fourth Republic

After the liberation of France from Nazi occupation in 1945, national elections were called with party lists and proportional representation. The electoral rules established in the constituent period 1945–6 included the d'Hondt formula of highest averages (which gives some advantage to larger parties). The ballot was an open list with candidates to be chosen from all parties or *panachage*. The rules admitted '*apparentments*', that is, electoral coalitions between parties running separately in order to allocate all seats in a district to the coalesced parties if their votes added up to an absolute majority (the seats would then be distributed among the winning parties proportionally to their votes).

These rules created incentives for forming broad electoral coalitions prefiguring further parliamentary and Cabinet multiparty coalitions. They were organized around the center, basically including the Socialists, the Radicals, the Christians, and the Conservatives, at the exclusion of the two extremes, the Communists and the Gaullists. The electoral rules permitted voters to select their most preferred individual candidates from the several parties in the coalition. An electoral reform in 1951 introduced additional mechanisms to reinforce the centrist moderation of the expected results. It established a quota formula of highest remainders for the districts in the Paris area in the aim of producing more proportional results and not giving advantage to the larger parties in that region, that is, the Communists and the Gaullists.

Of the six basic parties or blocs that were formed, usually the seats of four were necessary to form a majority in Parliament. The center-left Radicals were always the fifth in votes and in seats (if we take both the Radicals and the independent Conservative candidates as single groups). However, the Radicals always contained the median voter and the median seat and from this advantageous position they became the first party in number of Premiers and in number of Cabinet ministers.

In addition to the median, center-left Radicals, the left Socialists and the center-right Christians were also slightly advantaged in parliamentary bargaining and Cabinet formation because of their proximity to the median position on the policy-ideological space. In contrast, the extreme Communists and Gaullists, which, on average, were only slightly disadvantaged in terms of seats in comparison with their votes, were badly hurt in their expectations of being included in the Cabinet. Table 3.11 shows results in votes and seats, as well as in the further distribution of Cabinet ministers, for the five elections in the period 1945–56 (1945, June and November 1946, 1951, and 1956).

More specifically, the Cabinet coalitions during the constituent period 1945–7 were formed by the Communists, the Socialists, and the Christians with some minor participation on the part of Radicals (first, under the premiership of General de Gaulle and later mostly with Socialist premiers). However, from 1947 to 1958 the Communists were replaced with the Conservatives (also called 'Moderates'). Almost all premiers in this period were members of the more centrist parties within the typical four-party parliamentary coalition, the Radicals and the Christians. One exception in favor of a Conservative seems to have been based on voting miscalculation: the Radicals and the Christians voted for him in the expectation that he would not obtain sufficient votes, but unexpectedly some dissident Gaullists backed the candidate and made him a winner (Leites: 1959, p. 62).

The most common reproach to the French Fourth Republic was the instability of its Cabinets, which lasted only six months on average. Yet this can hardly be attributed to the electoral system of proportional representation and the corresponding multipartism, since a similar degree of Cabinet instability had existed in the previous French Third Republic with majoritarian electoral systems (based on plurality or majority rules). Almost all coalition Cabinets in the period 1875–1939 had been formed around the Republican Conservatives, mostly with the center-left Radicals as partners or, for some periods, the Christians. The Socialists were included in a governmental combination only in the period 1924–32 and in the short-lived experience of the Popular Front formed in 1936–38 by the Radicals, the Socialists, and the Communists. The average dura-

Table 3.11. *Votes, seats, and ministries in the French Fourth Republic (1945–58)*

		Votes	Seats	Ministries
LEFT	Communists	27	25	4
	Socialists	18	20	23
MEDIAN	Radicals	12	12	29
	Christians	20	22	25
	Conservatives	14	13	14
RIGHT	Gaullists	6	5	3
	Others	3	3	2
		100	100	100

Note: Numbers are percentages of votes, seats, and ministries for the five elections and twenty-five cabinets in the period 1945–58. Dotted lines separate Cabinet parties from more extreme or other parties.

Communists: PCF; Socialists: SFIO; Radicals: RGR, UDSR; Christians: MRP; Conservatives (or 'Moderates'): Independent Republicans, PRL, Paysans (PUS, IP); Gaullists: UG, RPF, ARS; Others: mainly 1956 'Poujadistes' (UFF).

Source: Author's own calculations with data in Williams (1958) and La Gorce (1979*a*,*b*).

tion of Cabinets in the period 1875–1939 was eight months; for the years 1918–39 it was six months, almost exactly the same length of time as for the period following 1945. (Soulier 1939). Despite Cabinet instability, the Third Republic represented by far the longest period of time in France since the fall of the absolutist Monarchy without a significant constitutional change and, as can be argued also for the Fourth Republic, a period of very stable policy.

The instability of Cabinets from 1946 ran in parallel to the long duration of the legislatures (five years in both 1946 and in 1951). This can be explained by a combination of institutional and strategic factors. The dissolution of the assembly was relatively difficult. The Cabinet could call anticipated elections only if two crises provoked by votes of censure or confidence had occurred within the preceding eighteen months. Since the threat of provoking dissolution and an anticipated election was hardly credible, individual ministers from parties in disagreement over some Cabinet policies dared to step down in the expectation of producing a new ministerial combination in which they might have more influence (Petry 1994).

Typically, the Premier and his Cabinet obtained support on the basis of proposals regarding some prominent issue, such as economic policy, European trade agreements, or colonial conflicts, and they were voted down as a consequence of a new divisive issue, such as the European Defence Community or the Church–school issue. The parties taking the initiative of overthrowing Cabinets were not the centrist Radicals or Christians, but those in less moderate positions in the ideological spectrum: the Socialists and the Conservatives, who were pulled towards the extremes by the challenging electoral strength of the Communists, the Gaullists, or the Poujadists. 'The parties that characteristically brought down the Cabinet did so for substantive [policy] reasons more than for calculations of places in future Cabinets, and suspicion that *ministrables* undermined the Cabinet [for office-seeking reasons] find little support in their votes' (MacRae 1967: 9, also 324).

These features reflected the general desire to keep the executive under control and to prevent power from residing in the hands of any one group in order to allow successive Cabinets to promote a variety of issues that would satisfy different group preferences. The effects of frequent reshuffles in favor of power redistribution could be compared to those sought by other institutional devices (such as the rotation in office by lots, as experimented with, for example, in some late medieval city-states), with the differential advantage of being produced under the stable framework of a five-year legislature and with co-responsibility within the four-party coalition.

All the Cabinets of the French Fourth Republic in the period 1945– 58 were supported by the parliamentary representatives of the median voter. Continuity in policy was favored by continuity in personnel: 15 individuals held 25 premierships, and 114 individuals held 411 ministerial portfolios (including the previously mentioned premierships), an average of 3.6 offices per person. For instance, the Christian-Democrat Robert Schuman was twice appointed Premier, ten times Minister of Foreign affairs, three times Minister of Finance, and twice Minister of Justice. Some parties or individuals kept certain ministries for long periods despite Cabinet changes, such as the Christians (Schuman and Bidault) in the Ministry of Foreign affairs, the independent Petsche in the Ministry of Finance, and the Socialists and the Radicals in the Ministry of the Interior (author's own calculation, which is very similar to the calculation of ministers and secretaries of state by Dogan 1989, who found an average of 3.4 offices per person).

The achievements of the French Fourth Republic include: the re-establishment of a democratic regime after the authoritarian rule of Marshal Pétain, and the War; dealing with the legacy of the German occupation while remaining one of the powers in the new diplomatic scenario; contributing to the European agreements on coal and steel, atomic energy, and the creation of the European Economic Community; negotiating independence for Tunisia and Morocco; ending the colonial war in Indo-China; and putting into play many long-term projects and legislation. During the Fourth Republic, France's economic recovery and development compared favorably with the rest of Europe. Paris was for a while a highly attractive international capital of the arts and humanities. Pluralistic intellectual life flourished, in contrast to further ideological polarization in the 1960s.

The French Fourth Republic ended as a result of a military coup. By early 1958, the French Army in Algeria began to act without the approval of the French

Cabinet by fighting against the movement for independence. In May, the Army chiefs removed civil officers in the colony and threatened to march on Paris in defence of a 'French Algeria'. General de Gaulle then quickly returned from political retirement and blackmailed the incumbent government with a military takeover if he were not given the premiership. The Gaullist party had obtained 22 per cent of votes in 1951 but its support had fallen to 4 per cent in the following election in 1956. The popular approval of the Premiers and Cabinets of the existing legislature elected in 1956 was as great as for the previous two legislatures (according to the collection of IFOP survey polls compiled by MacRae 1967: 309–13). Yet, under the threat of coup and in a highly unusual move, on June 1958 a majority of the National Assembly voted De Gaulle Premier and gave him special powers.

General de Gaulle eventually curbed the military rebellion and gave Algeria independence. At the same time, he introduced significant institutional changes which created a new Fifth Republic. On the one hand, Cabinet instability was reduced by increasing the requirements for a vote of censure and by giving the President of the Republic (de Gaulle himself) the power of dissolution of the Assembly. On the other hand, proportional representation in the National Assembly was replaced with majority rule. However, as discussed previously, political pluralism in France resisted the restrictive effects of the electoral reform and re-emerged strengthened. At the end of the 20th century, a five-party coalition Cabinet was 'cohabitating' with a President elected with the support of two other parties (one of them, in fact, a multiparty coalition itself).

The Italian First Republic

At the liberation of Italy from Fascism in 1945, national elections were called with party lists and proportional representation. The electoral rules established during the constituent period 1945–7 used the Imperiali quota at the district level and highest remainders at the national level, favoring the allocation of seats to parties according to their votes and the possibility for small parties to obtain parliamentary representation. The ballot admitted preferential vote for three or four individual candidates within a party list.

In the second election, in 1948, the Christian-Democratic party obtained an absolute majority of seats in the Chamber of Deputies with 48.5 per cent of votes. Then the Christians tried to introduce a new, majoritarian electoral rule that would have given two-thirds of seats to the party or electoral coalition of parties running separately that obtained an absolute majority of votes. Obviously, the Christians intended to consolidate their single-party domination with self-reinforcing rules. The electoral campaign of 1953 focused chiefly on this issue, with the opposition parties loudly denouncing 'the tricky law'. But the Christians did not obtain a majority of votes and proportional representation remained stable for the following forty years.

The Christian-Democratic party was dominant from 1946 to 1979. In eight successive elections it was the median voter party and, thanks to the proportionality of the electoral rules, it also captured the median seat in Parliament. The Communists were the second party in votes, but their extreme position on the left side of the ideological spectrum dramatically diminished their chance of entering into a majority parliamentary coalition. After the initial period of 'national concentration' governments (1945–7), the Communists were also vetoed as regular partners in national politics, especially for their position on Cold War foreign policy. The Christians, thus, could form frequent minority single-party Cabinets in the expectation that they would not be overthrown by a joint action of the parties on their left (basically Communists and Socialists) and on their right (Monarchists and Fascists). Alternatively, the Christians formed coalitions with minor partners of center-right, the Liberals, or center-left, the Republicans and the Social-Democrats. In 1963, the Socialists were also incorporated into multiparty coalition Cabinets with the Christians. After the election of 1976, even the Communists supported in Parliament the Cabinet of the Christian Premier Giulio Andreotti.

During this period, ministerial portfolios within multiparty Cabinets were distributed in rough proportion to each party's contribution in parliamentary seats to form a majority. But, as a consequence of frequent minority Cabinets of the Christians, these obtained in total about four times the number of ministries of the 'lay' parties combined despite having only about twice the number of seats of the latter (Socialists, Social-Democrats, Republicans, and Liberals). All premiers were members of the largest, median party.

A different period was initiated with the election of 1979. A higher proportion of votes for the Communists and a lower proportion for the Christians produced the effect of moving the median vote and the median seat to the 'lay' space, despite the fact that the parties in it had not broadened their electoral support.

From the new, advantageous median position, the 'lay' parties increased their bargaining power with the implicit threat of forming an alternative majority with the Communists (which in fact happened in a number of regional and local governments). Several four- and five-party coalition Cabinets were formed in this period. The Christians continued to have about twice the number of votes and parliamentary seats than all the 'lay' parties combined, but ministerial portfolios were now distributed exactly half-and-half from 1980 to 1992. Also, for about half this period the Premiers were members of minority parties, Giovanni Spadolini (1981–2), a Republican, and Bettino Craxi (1983–7), a Socialist. Table 3.12 shows results in notes and seats as well as in the further distribution of Cabinet ministers for the two periods mentioned.

The Christian-Democratic leadership developed formal rules for allocating ministries to both the parties and its own internal fractions according to some estimated value of the portfolios (the so-called 'Cencelli's manual'). Five categories of ministries were distinguished. The most important, A, included Foreign Affairs, Interior, and Finance, all of which were almost always controlled by the

TABLE 3.12. *Votes, seats, and ministries in the Italian First Republic (1945–92)*

		1945–79 (8 elections, 37 cabinets)				1979–92 (3 elections, 12 cabinets)		
		Votes	Seats	Ministries		Votes	Seats	Ministries
LEFT	Communists	25	26	<1		32	32	0
	'Lay' parties	21	18	15	*MEDIAN*	23	21	40
MEDIAN	Christians	40	44	76		35	38	53
	Liberals	4	4	3		2	2	4
RIGHT	Fascists	6	6	0		6	6	0
	Others	3	2	[5]		2	1	[3]
		100	100	100		100	100	100

Note: Numbers are percentages of votes, seats, and ministries. Dotted lines separate Cabinet parties from more extreme or other parties.

Communists: PCI and minor groups (PSIUP, LC, DP); 'Lay': Socialists (PSI), Social–Democrats (PSDI), Republicans (PRI), and Radicals (PR); Christians: DCI; Liberals: PLI; Fascists: Monarchists and MSI. 'Others' for ministries refer to independents.

Source: Author's own calculations with data in Furlong (1994).

Christians. The least important, D, included Tourism and Scientific Research the manual was published by Venditti 1981). In order to round off figures in the distributive calculus, the number of ministries in this period was increased from seventeen to thirty, with up to fifty-eight subsecretaries. Public banks, public companies, social security boards, social assistance agencies, and television channels were also apportioned. During this period the Parliament became gradually weaker, as can be illustrated by the increasing proportion of bills approved at the Cabinet's initiative. The governmental proposals were given a 'privileged path' and Parliament members' secret ballot was abolished in order to give the leaders control of party discipline. The Premier became a most powerful figure (Criscitiello 1994).

Italian politics during the First Republic (1945–92) has been characterized as having 'unstable Cabinets, relatively stable Ministers and Prime Ministers, lasting coalitions, and stagnating policies' (Pasquino 1996: 147). For extensive analyses supporting similar visions, see La Palombara 1987; Hine 1993.) There were eleven elections, thirty changes of premier, and forty-nine cabinets in forty-seven years. This means that the legislature lasted more than four years on average, while the average Cabinet duration was less than a year. Yet only nineteen individuals held the forty-nine Premierships, and seven of these did it for more than half the total time. In particular, Alcide De Gasperi was appointed Premier eight times (in the initial period 1945–53), Giulio Andreotti seven times, Amintore Fanfani six times, and Aldo Moro and Mariano Rumor five times each. All of them were Christian-Democrats. As mentioned, this party almost always controlled some crucial ministries, including those of the Interior, Foreign Affairs, Finance, Education, and Agriculture. Most reshuffles were negotiated by party leaders outside Parliament in order to avoid anticipated dissolution and elections. All of this produced a highly stable, moderate set of public policies from a socially efficient position of the Cabinets.

The First Italian Republic has on its record the re-establishment of a democratic regime after the Fascist period of Mussolini and World War II, its contribution to the creation of the European Economic Community, and a remarkable economic recovery and growth that made many observers speak of the 'Italian miracle'. A very long period of the same major party in power, however, fed clientelar relations between public administration and the ruling political parties, on one hand, and private companies on the other. Illegal private contributions to party finances obtained side-payments in policy decisions and other governmental favors. As mentioned, the executive powers expanded at the expense of parliamentary control, and interparty bargaining eventually distributed power away from the proportions of each party's electoral strength. In the 1992 election, people's support for the party system and certain aspects of the institutional framework had visibly eroded. Yet, it should be noted, contrary to some received opinion, that the decreasing performance of the Italian pluralistic democracy was not due to excessive governmental instability but rather to its opposite—the long-lasting, unchallenged power of the same rulers, a near immobilism.

As a result of baroque multiparty negotiations, the Chamber of Deputies was elected since 1994 with a new mixed system composed of single-member districts with plurality rule and multimember districts with proportional representation. It was expected that this system would promote a higher bipolarization leading to the displacement of the Christian-Democrats from government. Shaken by scandals concerning corruption and becoming the target of new decision rules and judicial prosecution, the Christian party indeed split into several factions, joining opposite electoral coalitions. Two large, heterogeneous multiparty blocs were formed, including as decisive partners the most extreme parties: reformed and unreformed Communists, on one side, and Populists and post-Fascists on the other. The moderate members of each bloc were much closer to each other than to their extreme partners. The two blocs quickly alternated in government in the second half of the 1990s.

Yet, against most expectations, the newly fractionalized political center, approximately corresponding to the legacy of the Christian and the 'lay' parties, was able to develop significant bargaining power. Under the new rules, the small, centrist parties obtained some seats on the basis of proportional representation. At the same time, they could threaten the larger parties of the left and the right with the prospect of running separately in the single-member districts with the aim of making the plurality winner dependent on irrelevant alternatives. As a result of this threat and the corresponding bargaining power, the divided centrist parties were given significant proportions of likely winning candidacies within each of the two large multiparty electoral coalitions. Political pluralism in Italy thus strongly resisted the restrictive effects of the electoral reform of the 1990s. At the end of the 20th century, there were more parties in Parliament than ever before and the incumbent Cabinet was a seven-party coalition.

The Netherlands: From Accommodation to Compromise

In 1918, at the end of World War II, universal suffrage and proportional representation were introduced in the Netherlands. A relatively high number of political parties already existed at that time. The electoral system in use since then is based on a single countrywide district and allocation of seats to parties on the basis of a combination of their quotas of votes and the d'Hondt formula of largest averages. This system produces extremely proportional results and has allowed about four or five major parties to be represented in the Lower House (with up to 14 parties in total in the early 1970s).

The present survey starts after the parenthesis produced by World War II, although major elements of continuity with the previous period can be identified. The major political parties of the Netherlands were initially organized along two different issue-dimensions. First, one Catholic and two major Calvinist parties gave high salience to religious and moral issues. Until the 1963 election, the religious parties together collected a majority of votes and seats in the Lower House. Second, the left, led by the Socialists, and the right, formed by the Liberals, were defined and split on economic issues. Each of the two sets of parties, the religious bloc and the Socialist-Liberal set, gave prominence to different issues and obtained the support of different groups of voters. There was no real competition between the two sets of parties on the same issues nor significant amounts of shifting voters.

During the first twenty years after World War II, the fragmentation of the policy-issue space, as well as the existence of several religious parties, led to the formation of broad multiparty coalitions. All Cabinets included parties with clearly defined positions on each of the two issue-dimensions, which made room for numerically superfluous partners to enter the corresponding coalitions. They were always formed by the Christians together with either the Socialists or the Liberals, or both. This period was the basis for Arend Lijphart's elaboration of his model of 'the politics of accommodation'. Surplus coalitions and consensus politics were presented as essential features of this Dutch-inspired model (Lijphart 1968).

The religious dimension lost prominence in the political agenda and the religious parties ceased to gather together a majority of votes and seats after the election of 1967. The three Christian parties previously alluded to eventually merged into a single candidacy in 1977 and a single party in 1980 (the Christian

Democratic Appeal, or CDA). At the same time, new minor 'lay' parties emerged. The left–right axis became the main organizing dimension of the party system on which all parties tended to compete. Electoral competition and the volatility of voters' choices increased (Irwin and van Holsteyn 1989*a*, *b*).

This new situation created some opportunities for higher bipolarization. As a result, the Socialists and the Radicals (Democrats '66) promoted some institutional reforms, including a majoritarian electoral system, in order to facilitate more drastic alternations of parties in government. When these reforms were rejected by the Christians and the Liberals, the Socialists developed a confrontational strategy by forming a common front with two minor radical parties as a commitment to support a more left-oriented Cabinet after the election if they obtained a sufficient number of seats. However, this strategy by the Socialists backfired. In fact, it induced the Christians and the Liberals to respond by choosing each other as preferred Cabinet partners to the exclusion of the Socialists, a coalition which was predominant in the second half of the 1970s and 1980s.

The majority support of the Christian parties, initially, and their central position on the left–right dimensions later, gave them some global advantage in forming governments for fifty years, as reflected in the higher proportion of ministries than shares of votes and seats they controlled. New Cabinet formulas emerged in more recent times, including the one formed by the Socialists and the Liberals. Most Cabinets since 1967 have been based on minimum-winning coalitions without numerically superfluous partners, but there has been a considerable rotation of parties in all ministries and a general sense of compromise when it comes to establishing major public policies (Daalder 1986, 1989). Table 3.13 shows results in volts and seats, as well as in the futher distribution of Cabinet ministers in the period 1946–98.

Cabinet formation is usually a lengthy and laborious process in the Netherlands. Multiparty negotiations may take several months from the election day to completion (with the record at 207 days in 1977). These negotiation costs, a couple of shifting coalitions during the legislature of 1963–7, and some unpredictability of the exact party composition of Cabinets on the basis of the electoral results, moved some politicians and opinion leaders to underline the negative aspects of the consensus politics model and to favor clearer choices. In the 1970s, even Arend Lijphart temporarily suspected that accommodation would be replaced with more adversarial politics (as discussed in Lijphart 1989).

However, the full panorama of Dutch politics since 1945 shows a very high degree of Cabinet and policy stability, moderation, and social efficiency. Post-electoral negotiations are open rather than 'smoke-filled'. Sixty per cent of Cabinets completed their legal terms, the average duration being more than thirty months. Only twelve Premiers led twenty-one Cabinets in fifty-five years, some with long stays in power, such as the Socialist W. Drees for ten years (1948–58) and the Christian R.F.M. Lubbers for twelve years (1982–94). From the point of view of its accomplishments in a growing economy and social well-being, the